"Spain is still a country mercifully free of petty rules and stifling regulations. If someone wants to run in front of a bull, wrestle a wild horse to the ground, or hurl fireworks ... If it's fiesta time, anything goes." *Benjamin Curtis*

Packed with ideas, inspiration and 'travel intelligence' on Spain from top writers and journalists - hotels, hideaways, restaurants, walks, sights and much more - the BEST OF SPAIN is your first step to rediscovering the magic of Spain. Detailed planning chapters on websites, books and specialist operators follow each section. Whether you are a first time visitor or an experienced traveller, our aim is to stimulate new ways to get the most from this favourite destination.

Some of these articles, as well as thousands of others, can be seen online at WWW.TRAVELINTELLIGENCE.NET

Anthology copyright © 2002 Travel Intelligence Ltd. All written material authors' copyright. For image and additional credits, see final page.

Travel Intelligence Ltd does not guarantee the accuracy or suitability of any advice given in this publication, and cannot be held liable for any errors or omissions. You are strongly advised to check practical details in advance of making travel plans, because these can change frequently and without warning.

Further titles in this series:
The Best of France
The Best of Italy

Edited, with section introductions, by
**Benjamin Curtis**
Series Editor / Designer
**Jamie Dunford Wood**
Editorial Director
**AA Gill**
Assistant Editor
**Lucy Judkins**
Editorial Assistants
**Jenny Pidgeon**
**Allyson Benavidez**

## Travel Intelligence contributing writers

Alf ALDERSON   Sarah ANDERSON   Rose BARING   Maureen BARRY   Richard BINNS   Dea BIRKETT   John BORTHWICK   Greg BREINING   Tom BROSNAHAN (commissioning editor, US)   Sue CARPENTER   David CLEMENT-DAVIES   Joe CUMMINGS   Ben CURTIS   William DALRYMPLE   Andrew EAMES   Catherine FAIRWEATHER   AA GILL (editorial director)   Robin HANBURY-TENISON   Justine HARDY   Fraser HARRISON   John HATT   Anthony HEALY   James HENDERSON   Mark HUDSON   Rupert ISAACSON   Brian JACKMAN   Steve JERMANOK   Tom KAY   Jim KEEBLE   Steven KNIPP   Nancy LYON   Rory MACLEAN   Philip MARSDEN (commissioning editor, UK)   Lee MARSHALL   Gregory McNAMEE   Mark MCCRUM   Kamin MOHAMMADI   Kate MORRIS   Andrew MUELLER   Martin O'BRIEN   Rob PENN   Barnaby ROGERSON   Melissa ROSSI   Anthony SATTIN   Dan SCOTT   Jeremy SEAL   Jasper SHARP   Christopher SOMERVILLE   Rory SPOWERS   Lucretia STEWART   Stanley STEWART   Susan STORM   Sean THOMAS   Nigel TISDALL   Isabella TREE   Yvonne VAN DONGEN   Vitali VITALIEV   Binyavanga WAINAINA   John WARBURTON-LEE   Sara WHEELER   Simon WINCHESTER   Jasper WINN   Stuart WOLFENDALE

# The Best of Spain

ISBN 1-904131-07-7

published by Travel Intelligence Ltd
2 Oaklands Grove, London W12 0JA United Kingdom

For information on **Travel Intelligence**'s other products and services, please visit **www.travelintelligence.net** or email i@travelintelligence.net

# CONTENTS

# Introduction

BY Benjamin Curtis

You hear the same thing over and over in Madrid.

*"I only came for a week ...a fortnight ....a month, and I've been here ever since."*

All over Spain there are people who came, saw something different, something better, and, given the freedom to do so, stayed here for good. What they saw was a country that is markedly different from all the rest, a country that is so far removed from the popular image of the package-holiday 'costas', that it makes you want to go down to those crowded sunny beaches and drag the idle holidaymakers around the 'real Spain' by the scruffs of their necks.

But that would be missing the point. Benidorm, Marbella and Tossa de Mar are as real and as Spanish as you can get. Not only that, but the Spanish love them just as much as the tourists do. They are all just part of the giant, swinging pendulum that is Spain, a land of infinite opposites. Just behind those seething sun-tan coasts lie silent, shimmering Sierras, decked out in vineyards and olive groves.

Pick any two points, in fact, on the giant Spanish peninsular and diversity leaps out at you. Whilst it's pouring with spring rain in deep-green Asturias, you may find yourself driving through the wild-west hills of Almeria, in

5

blinding sunlight, stopping to look at the film sets where many of the spaghetti westerns were filmed. Half an hour later, down on the deserted Cabo de Gata coast, you might bet a friend that you can find a scorpion under a rock, then find three in a row. In summer they still scythe the hay by hand on the steeper slopes of the Picos de Europa, whilst just over the border in Galicia, the trawlers are bringing in fishing catches of industrial proportions. In the province of Madrid you can ski in December on pine-covered slopes, then drop down to the capital an hour later for all the commodities of a raging city. Soria in winter can be at ten degrees below zero, whilst down in Cadiz they bask in 20 degree sunshine.

This diversity has led to the catchy concept of 'different Spains', though we can just as easily talk about 'different Spaniards'. The Catalans dislike the Madrilenos (who call the Catalans tight-fisted in return), the Galicians fight to give their dialect the same level of recognition as, say, the Basques have for their own ancient language, the same Basques who enjoy unprecedented levels of cultural, fiscal and political autonomy. The country is united in division, just as it has always been, swinging back and forth through history, one dynasty after another, hardly a historical pause for breath between one bloody hand-over and the next. The twentieth century alone saw a monarchy, a republic, a vicious civil war, Franco the dictator, the rise of democracy and the return of the monarchy, and another attempted coup as late as the eighties.

It was then, as tanks rolled onto the streets of Valencia, that King Juan Carlos had to step in to safeguard the fledgling democracy. At El Escorial, incidentally, you can visit half a millennium of this same king's predecessors. They lie in vast marble coffins inside the Royal mausoleum, just past the ante room where his mother is currently "putrefying" - so the guides will tell you.

Through all this diversity runs a striking simplicity. The less pretentious the food, for example, the more highly it is valued. No haute-cuisine will ever come close to giving the pleasure derived form a full plate of thinly sliced "Jamon Iberico", eaten on a sunny terraza, and washed down with a glass of Rioja. There is a simplicity in the siesta (that everyone still takes at weekends), and there is something heart-warmingly simple about the countryside, about turning off onto a winding B-road, or wandering down an aromatic mountain path, Don Quixote-like, imagination poised, in search of adventures.

A few years ago I came to Madrid for a month, and I stayed. I found a city where you could go out all night without anyone telling you when to drink up and go home, a city where asking for directions could easily elicit a polite, considered, two minute explanation. Everyone seemed to be in a reasonably good mood most of the time, and the sun shone, undisturbed, for thirty days in a row. Life was lived on the streets, yet even in the most exasperated rush-hour crowds, or amongst the largest groups of drunken teenagers, it was almost impossible to find a trace of metropolitan hostility. Madrid represented a quality of life that was definitely worth living. How well, then, does the capital represent its nation. As you wander around the country you soon discover that perhaps this, beyond all that simplicity and diversity, is what best defines Spain: it is a way of life, led in a wonderful collection of breath-taking landscapes, and for the most part bathed in glorious sunshine.

THINGS TO DO 'BEFORE YOU DIE' No. 207

*Seville*
"Enjoy the tapas bars in Seville on Thursday nights in February, before the weekenders come in, when the young Sevillanos are just strutting their stuff and the orange blossom smells very strong." *Justine Hardy*

# City Spain

# City Spain

The rise of the low-cost internet airlines has opened up Spain as an ideal city-break location. Flight times of two to three hours mean accessible trips to cities like Alicante, Jerez, Malaga and Bilbao. Travelling mid-week brings prices tumbling even further. Madrid and Barcelona are the obvious targets, the former for a treasure trove of art, late nights and a taste of the wild life, the latter for Gaudi and vibrant, cosmopolitan beach life. But what about escaping the obvious, and using the budget destinations as a gateway to a far more Spanish, tourist-free experience?

Alicante, for example, is a fascinating city with good beaches and an interesting old town. Bus an hour down the motorway, however, past orange groves and sparkling sea views, and you'll hit Valencia, a far more appetising destination. This salty Mediterranean city is a peculiar combination of ancient crumbling streets, often as tight as corridors, airy plazas shaded by palms and giant Banyan trees, bright new architecture, giant paellas, lively night life and, outside March's Las Fallas festivities, hardly a fellow tourist to be seen.

Similarly, flying to Barcelona opens up Tarragona, a uniquely Catalan city with fascinating Roman archeological remains. Malaga is just a hop from Granada, the perfect luxury weekend destination, as James Henderson explains below. Jerez opens up the sherry triangle completed by the swarthy southern cities of Sanlucar and El Puerto de Santa Maria, and is just twenty minutes from the exotic, fallen glory of Cadiz. If you're flying to Bilbao, by all means do the Guggenheim, but give the rest of the city a miss and head on to the stately sea-side splendours of San Sebastian. In Avila, Segovia, and Toledo, all a brief hire-car ride from Madrid's Barajas airport, you will find the very essence of Spain.

Finally, if you are not constrained by cheap-flight destinations, a handful more cities deserve special consideration. Salamanca, a gentle city sculpted in sandstone and marooned on the plains, was once host to the greatest university in Europe. Burgos, frozen solid in winter, stifling in summer, has beautiful tree-lined river walks, and the most beautiful cathedral in Spain. Lastly, Santiago de Compostela, with a mighty cathedral of its own, is a city from another time, of wide open plazas, delectable seafood and delicate rain, all set in blocks of granite, beneath the field of stars that gave it its name.

# James Henderson

---

## GRANADA - A LUXURY WEEKEND

It is easy to see why the Moor sighed as he was forced to leave Granada.

It is a city of magnificent views. In the startling southern Spanish light, the towers of the Alhambra shimmer against the backdrop of the Sierra Nevada and the whitewashed carmens of Granada's Arab quarter stack invitingly on the steep hillside. Granada is also resonant with romance, having fired the imagination of Romantic poets and painters two centuries ago. More recently Bill Clinton brought Hillary here especially to see the sunset.

The city has long since lost its importance - it was the last Moorish kingdom in Spain and then, with the Reconquista, became the capital of the new Spain under Catholic Monarchs Ferdinand and Isabella - but now the gentle apotheosis of Arab culture in Spain has subsided into quiet and charm, a self-possessed provincial town. It is accessible, though; easy to acquaint yourself with in a long weekend. Granada's pleasures are mostly within walkable distance, but it is hilly, so you may choose to ride up and walk down.

Start at the top of the old Arab quarter, the Albaicin, where a network of tight cobbled alleys weave among the city's carmens, walled houses and gardens with vine-shaded terraces. As you descend, look out for the elaborate wrought-iron gates and window grilles, the town's brightly coloured tiles in door-frames, or a sudden moorish arch. Briefly the alleys open into placetas and miradors, from where the view extends for miles.

But the views are not all massive. Lower down you will find outer doors ajar. Sneak a look as you pass: into elaborately tiled entraditas or vestibules and then beyond, through interior doors to courtyards laid with marble flagstones where fountains play among huge earthenware urns cascading with flowers.

At the foot of the Albaicin you come to the axis of the modern town, the grandiose Gran Via de Colon (Columbus: as well as the Reconquista, 1492 was the year that Columbus discovered America for Spain). Beyond is the Capilla Real, where the marble tombs of Ferdinand and Isabella, her head weighing more heavily on the pillow because of her superior intellect, lie behind a magnificent reja or gilded grille. Do not miss the sacristy with the military pennants of the Reconquista, tapestries worked by Isabella and her superb collection of paintings by Memling, Botticelli and Dirk Bouts. As you leave, dip into the Palacio de la Madraza for a view of Moorish delights to come tomorrow.

Nearby, the Cathedral has lumpen massiveness, but you should visit for the baroque finery of the side-altars and for two small statues in the museum (by Alonso de Cano, the Cathedral's architect), of the Madonna and child and St Paul. For a late afternoon break, the Arab tea-houses on the Calderia Arabe offer a mint or jasmin infusion and in early evening people repair to the balcony at the Alhambra Palace Hotel, where the city's noise reduces to a tiny roar.

You may want to test Granada's evening shopping: Calles Zacatin, Mesones and Alhondiga are near the Cathedral. Leatherwear is well priced, particularly shoes. The Alcaiceria alley offers Arab-inspired crafts including silver jewellery, but for marquetry (elaborate boxes and backgammon boards of inlaid woods) you should go to the Cuesta de Gomerez or the Alhambra complex. On Calle Elvira there are dusty, den-like antique shops. Granada is known for its ceramics: visit the San Isidro showroom on Plaza Isidro or the two rival Fajalauza factories on the Carretera de Murcia above the Albaicin.

Some of Granada's restaurants make the best of the magnificent views: in the window seats of the Carmen de San Miguel, you hover over the town, looking up to the Sierra Nevada (gazpacho and Granadian fish casserole, neatly presented) and from the wood and tiled interior or vine-covered terraces of the Mirador de Morayma, there is a magnificent view of the Alhambra; good local ajo blanco, garlic soup with almonds and shredded apple, or Remojon salad - codfish, orange and black olives. In the stylish El Galatino on the Gran Via you dine to the quiet clink of cutlery beneath trompe-l'oeil walls and earthy plasterwork. Try a hefty local lomo de buey (ox steak) or shellfish ragout.

But you need not sit down to a formal meal in Granada. The bars have their speciality tapas. The Plaza Nueva is a lively area as is the Carretera del Darro running along the river. Also try Calle Navas, off the Plaza de Carmen. Castaneda has excellent local Alpujarra ham. For something a little more local, you can try the bars in the Albaicin: El Aixa, known for its migas, Torcuato and El Aliatar, which presents you with snails served in a rich, spicy sauce, to be winkled out with a toothpick. If you are peckish for something sweet, the best shop is Bernina, down below on the Plaza de Carmen.

The Alhambra is the most visited monument in Europe and entry is limited to 400 each half hour, but visits can be booked in advance. Private guides are very expensive unless they can be shared, but they can book your tickets.

True to Arab form, the outer walls are drab, but inside the rooms and patios of the Casa Real are exquisitely adorned with patterned tiles, a forest of slender columns supporting rounded arches and a filigree of mixed alabaster and plaster. Ceilings are pointed with stucco as papery and delicate as a wasps' nest. And of course there are the views, looking out from inside and vice versa, and out over the town. The finest is in the Courtyard of the Myrtles, where seven arches stand reflected in a long rectangular pool. Amid this flighty beauty and the gardens of the Generalife, attached to the nearby summer palace, King Charles V's renaissance palace feels as though it is muscling in.

Though most of the city's carmens are private, some have become hotels. By far the most elegant place to stay in Granada is the Carmen de los Chapiteles - between them, the King and Queen of Spain and the Spice Girls can't be wrong - but it must be booked as a unit, all five bedrooms. On the Alhambra hill itself, the finest rooms in the Parador de San Francisco are around the exquisite interior courtyard, which retains some of the tranquility of the monastery it once was (other areas see a constant through-flow of inquisitive visitors). Down below, a couple of hotels have pretty interior courtyards; the Palacio de Santa Ines in the lower Albaicin, with sixteenth century murals, and the Reina Cristina.

It is only really possible to see Flamenco in a show. Try Jardines Neptuno. There are also shows in Sacromonte, the old gypsy quarter outside the city walls (itself worth a quick look, though there are 'more Germans then gypsies' now): try Cueva los Tarantos.

But beware: Granada gets crowded in summer,

especially at Corpus Christi in early June during the week of bullfighting, and during Granada's Festival of arts in late June and early July. Like all the most popular cities, be prepared to come out of season.

# Benjamin Curtis

## Letter From San Sebastian

The moment you leave Spain's sun-baked central high plateau and descend north-east into the topsy-turvy, bottle-green hills of the Basque Country, you may feel a certain sympathy for the locals who argue for a separate, liberated Basque nation of their own. Not for the bomb-throwing terrorists or teenage weekend rioters, but for the family living at the head of one of these great valleys in an ancient farmhouse whose white-washed walls could not be further from Madrid's centralised government if they were on the other side of the world.

The Basque Country, brooding away from Bilbao to Biarritz, quite simply doesn't look Spanish. It's just too green, soft and fecund to be associated with the harsher extremes that constitute the rest of Spain. It looks like a landscape adrift, snagged up on the wrong side of Europe, exiled from some distant mountainous home.

I'm spending a night in San Sebastian, the burning heart of Basque nationalist sentiments, on my way to France. I wouldn't be stopping at all if I'd listened to the dissenting voices in Madrid. "They burn buses there every weekend", I heard, "The old town is very dangerous", and time and again, "A beautiful city, but what a shame about the 'problems'". Any mention of these 'problems', similar to Northern Ireland's Troubles, causes a lot of mystified head shaking in Madrid, and is usually exaggerated to the extreme.

Once you arrive, however, it's hard to imagine that there

are any problems here. You'll find little more than a supremely elegant, work-a-day city, a small fishing fleet, and, to my mind, the most beautiful urban beaches in the world. The best way to appreciate them, and the city itself, is on foot - a good couple of hours' stroll end to end.

San Sebastian sits proudly against the Atlantic coast, clustered around two horseshoe bays separated by a central headland. The easterly beach, Gros, is a fine place to start. Littered with young, bronzed bodies in summer, for the rest of the year it resumes its roll as a wide, wind-blown, sandy city park, home to dog walkers, joggers and all-weather surfers, who travel far for the city's famous breaks.

This beach's most distinguished feature is "El Kursaal", a gigantic architectural experiment. Two cuboid conference centre monsters in steel and sky-grey glass perch on the beach, blocking certain irate flat-owners' views of the sea. This is San Sebastian's answer to Bilbao's Guggenheim; finished in 1999, it is said to reflect "the romance between the city and the sea".

"Do people like it?" I ask a local girl. "They have to!" she replies, "what else can they do?"

Winner of many an architectural prize, the building's design is said to be based on the beach's sea defences, vast blocks stretching out to sea, cut, at goodness knows what expense, from local marble. In other seaside cities concrete blocks would normally do.

Heading on west you'll first cross the city river where fishermen line the bridges and men with buckets scour the rocks for shellfish at low tide. The central headland that separates the two bays is home to the old town, a warren of tall apartment buildings and tight cobbled streets. Hanging from every corner is the colourful Union Jack-like 'Ikurriña', the Basque national flag. Any of the bars here will serve up the most refined Tapas in Spain, known locally as 'Pinchos', to be taken at will from mouth-watering bar-top platefuls and washed down with young, fizzy 'Txakolin' wine. Eat and drink as much as you like, keeping a mental count as you go, then pay up before you leave. One can only imagine how much a system like this would be abused at home.

Leaving the old town again, worn down by the gourmet delights within, you emerge by the harbour, gazing onto La Concha beach, jewel in San Sebastian's fading crown: a lazy curve of golden sand backed by an elegant promenade, protected from the ocean by an abrupt, molar-like central island, and lorded over by the bay's personal dolphin. In autumn the local schools organise Rugby matches on the soft sand at low tide. This the stuff of Harry Potter and his magical games of 'Quidditch' compared to the miserable, frozen British playing fields that I once knew.

Don't give up once you've got this far but keep going right round to the very end of the bay, past the tennis club and the funicular railway leading up to a crumbling amusement park. Here, at the point where the road ends and the cliffs rise dramatically away from the sea, are Eduardo Chillida's 'Combs of the wind' - three twisted, rusting fingers of solid sculpted iron, one jutting straight out from the cliff, the others erupting seamlessly from great outcrops of bronzed rock that protrude from the sea. The work is awe-inspiring, ensnaring the elements that surround it and feeding them back into the city behind.

I spend the night in the company of some Basques who tell me, ironically after what I'd heard in the capital, how much they'd love to go and live in Madrid. Before I leave the following morning I pick up a copy of the local paper, the

'Diario Vasco', and take a last walk along Gros beach. Sand, sea, horizon and sky are static, blending into one, the air cool and salty. I'm sorry to leave this regal old city, the indomitable Queen of the Basque court, but have to head north into France.

Later, somewhere near Bordeaux, I open my paper and am surprised to find the headline "Bus Burning in San Sebastian." The previous afternoon, just before I arrived, four youths in balaclavas boarded a bus and obliged its occupants, at axe handle-point, to leave, before throwing various Molotov cocktails into the back. One person was treated for shock. Fire-fighters extinguished the flames but had not been able to save the bus. I decided not to mention this to anyone when I got back to Madrid. I wouldn't want the prejudices that keep them, and consequently others, away from the delights of the Basque country, to be strengthened by the idea that they'd been right all along.

# City Planning

## Recommended Reading

**Madrid - Time Out Guide**
Penguin Publications. ISBN: 0140293876

**Barcelona**
By Robert Hughes. Panther. ISBN: 1860468241

**Lorca's Granada**
by Ian Gibson. Faber and Faber. ISBN: 0571164897

**Spain: Granada, Seville and Cordoba**
By Dana Facaros, Michael Pauls. Cadogan Guides.
ISBN: 1860118267

## General Web Resources

**spainalive.com**
Spain Alive's strength lies in giving the kind of reliable up-to-date information that you can usually only get when you arrive, covering local events, restaurants, night life, shopping and accommodation, especially for Valencia, Madrid, Barcelona and Seville.

**red2000.com**
This site provides an A-Z index with details on nearly every city in Spain. The most popular destinations include photographs, and detailed descriptions of local sights, cultural activities and fiestas. The site also links to a comprehensive database of hotels and accommodation all over Spain.

**tourspain.es**
This web site, created by the Spanish Tourist Board, provides a
wealth of information on Spain, including a good, factual round up
of the most interesting cities on the Peninsular.

**paisvasco.com**
An excellent site with tourist information and accommodation for
San Sebastian - Donestia in Basque.

## Travel Specialists

### Mundi Color
Apart from covering the best-known cities, Mundi Color also offers
short breaks to less obvious destinations such as Salamanca,
Segovia, Toledo, Avila, Cuenca, Zaragoza and Jerez.
mundicolor.co.uk; Tel: 020 7828 6021

### The Magic of Spain
This company specialises not only in carefully chosen hotels in the
major cities (Bilbao, Valencia, Madrid...), but also offers tours that
include stays in an impressive variety of historical, provincial cities
such as Merida, Caceres, Zamora and Leon.
magictravelgroup.co.uk; Tel: 08700 270 480

### Travellers Way
This is a good bet if you are looking for a touring holiday, or
hoping to combine a trip to Madrid with smaller Castillian cities
such as Salamanca, Avila, Segovia, Burgos, Cuenca or Toledo.
travellersway.co.uk; Tel: 01527 578000

## Accommodation: Hotels of Interest

Quite often it's worth visiting a city for a hotel alone. A good
selection, with independent reviews, can be found at

travelintelligence.net, but below are some of our favourites:

**San Sebastian:** The Maria Cristina (Tel: +34 943 424900) matches any hotel in Spain for pure five star luxury, though I might opt in preference for the Hotel de Londres y de Inglaterra (Tel: +34 943 426989), for its old fashioned charm and front-row views over La Concha beach.

**Madrid:** If money is no option it must be the Ritz (Tel: +34 91 5212857), otherwise, for slightly less, try the elegantly discreet Hotel Santo Mauro (Tel: +34 91 3196900), a centrally located, five star establishment with pool.

**El Puerto de Santa Maria:** Hidden amongst the criss-cross streets of the purely Andalucian old town, the Monasterio de San Miguel was once a convent. This beautiful hotel has rooms over-looking fountain-filled courtyards, and a soporific pool-side bar. (Tel: +34 956540404)

**Toledo and Segovia:** Sometimes the key to a remarkable hotel is its view. Here, the state-run, luxury Parador chain (parador.es) has excelled itself in terms of location, commanding stunning views over each of these two cities.

**Granada:** James Henderson mentions the Hotel Reina Cristina (Tel: +34 958 253211); the Hotel Palacio de Santa Ines (Tel: +34 958 222342); the Carmen de los Chapiteles (+34 958 220177) and the Parador de San Francisco (+34 958 221440).

## Getting There

**Iberia:** Regular flights direct from London Airports to Alicante, Barcelona, Madrid, Malaga, Oviedo, Seville, Santaigo de Compostella and Valencia; iberia.com; Tel: 08456 012854

**British Airways:** Scheduled service to Madrid, Barcelona, Bilbao, Santiago de Compostela and Seville; britishairways.com; Tel: 0845 77 333 77

**British Midlands:** Discount flights from East Midlands airport to Alicante, Barcelona and Malaga; bmibaby.co.uk

**Buzz:** Discount flights to Murcia and Jerez. buzzaway.com

**GB Airways:** Scheduled services to Valencia; gbairways.com; Tel: 01293 664239

**Go:** Discount flights to Malaga, Bilbao and Barcelona; gofly.com

**EasyJet:** Discount flights to Madrid, Malaga and Barcelona; easyjet.com; Tel: 0870 6 000 000

# Gastronomic Spain

# Gastronomic Spain

The Spaniard might happily dismiss all international cuisine, but they will happily discuss, for hours, which village does the best bean stew, or which take-away joint the best spit-roast chicken. When it comes to food and drink, they are fearfully proud. Although the same dishes crop up again and again all over the country, every family will have a favourite bar for prawns, a particular restaurant for lamb. Perhaps this pride is a legacy of the great famine that swept the country during Franco's reign, but more likely it's for the same reason that the Spanish rarely holiday abroad: why look elsewhere when everything you need is on your doorstep?

Though some travellers may be upset by roast suckling piglet (must be eaten in Segovia), or steer clear of long, tubular Goose Barnacles ('percebes' - only in Galicia), Spanish food generally consists of basic ingredients, prepared unpretentiously: good meat, simple vegetables and an unsurpassable range of fresh fish and seafood (all prepared in Andalucian olive oil). Always find out what the local speciality is, and you'll soon see why the Spanish have no need to import foreign cuisine.

Meal times are amongst the latest in Europe. Lunch, the main meal of the day, never starts before two, and may last until at least five. Look out for bars and restaurants that do a 'menu del dia' at lunchtime, an incredible value, all-inclusive three course lunch. Supper generally happens from ten onwards and tends to be lighter, sometimes just a few tapas. In many regions, and to excess in Granada, these will be given free with every drink in a bar.

A great place for tapas, as Melissa Rossi discovers below, is Madrid. The capital, however, has other gourmet attractions for the traveller. The city may lie slap-bang in the middle of Spain, but is paradoxically famous for the finest and freshest fish you can imagine, hauled up every night of the week from distant coastal ports. Here, too, you can eat your way through every region in Spain: a hearty lunch of beans and beef at an Asturian 'Cidreria', then octopus and fiery Padron peppers for supper at a Galician 'Meson.'

If, however, you prefer to eat regional cooking in its region of origin, then two areas stand out above the rest. Galicia's seafood is amongst the best in the world, second only, some say, to that found in Nova Scotia. Such is the range of fresh produce brought in by the boats every day, that Spaniards from other parts of the country often have trouble recognising items on the menu. Secondly, the Basque Country not only has some of the best presented, most imaginative, wholesome and conscientiously prepared cuisine in Europe, but also boasts the country's most famous restaurant, Arzak in San Sebastian.

Spain is now producing a phenomenal array of high-quality wines. Beyond the famous Riojas, Ribera del Duero and Toro are emerging as leading names in red wine, whilst Rueda is the label to seek out for white. 'Fino', or the lighter

'Manzanilla', shouldn't be sniffed at in Andalucia. Served cold they are incredibly refreshing, and far more refined than the 'sherry' you'll know from home. Locally produced liqueurs such as the fiery, clear Orujo, or Pacharan, are usually drunk after meals, though for spirits, it's often safer to stick to foreign 'importacion' brands than those produced in Spain. One long term ex-pat reported giving up a certain Spanish whisky after discovering that a few glasses always caused him to lose all his clothes.

# David Clement-Davies

A Flavour of the Campo

I'm failing to penetrate the dark interior of Andalucían cooking - to bring back, like a portly Conquistador, the culinary wealth of Granada, Seville and Jerez. I'd meant to sweep down off my hilltop into Malaga, to the liveliest seafood restaurant in town, where they auction the dishes, platter by glistening platter. Or drive west to Antequera, where you can dine in the awnings of the Bullring, and guzzle steak to your heart's content.

But I don't want to do anything but gaze, silent upon a peak... Light rain has made the hills of Arxarquía look like a miniature Peru. Breathtakingly clear days have everything in brilliant focus; poplars turning chestnut-gold, the crack of a rabbit gun down the valley, the cloud topped slopes of the Sierra Tejeda. From here you can almost see to Africa, and even the endless olive groves look interesting. And I've never had the slightest interest in olives.

That's obviously absurd in Spain so, dutiful to the last, I've found out that you can only harvest the angry, bitter little fruits once every two years, and green and black grow on the same tree. Well, it's a portion of the meagre fare I can share with you, along with my shopping list. I mention the supermarket only to balance out the romance, because it's there that you taste the horrors of the Costa del Crime, 40 minutes away. Forget the Supertanker holiday apartments or Spanglesa, the Andalucian equivalent of Franglais; blush at the Helmann's Mayonnaise, Cranberry Jelly, Brown Sauce and McVities digestive biscuits, stacked in over-loud abundance.

Trying to brush England aside I lit a wood fire in my house and attempted to cook 'autentico' on my farmer's griddle. It was a charming idyll, until the sitting room disappeared under a spitting carbon cloud and I found my cutlets so rusticated I could only serve them to Mowgli, the always appreciative black mongrel. Mowgli has to snuffle around for anything he can get up here so admittedly, he's no judge.

Mind you, in terms of food, I'm not entirely sure Arxarquia isn't a region as mythical as El Dorado. Down at the bar, Raphelito's aubergines with honey are excellent, but limp chips draped with lemon slices can hardly compare to El Rincon which I read, with twinges of frustration, is already raising a red cape to bullish London restaurateurs.

Undeterred, I set out all of twenty yards to ask at the bar. I thought it was heroic, challenging four such rugged chins with a question like "what's the speciality of the campo?" If you ever want a signifier of Andalucian manhood, just stop in a petrol station and buy a motoring pack of 'Decorative Lingerie', (pink bra or blue knickers) instead of the furry dice, to hang over the rear view mirror.

But lo and behold - Ortega y Gazet - the whole swarthy crowd donned their metaphorical pinnies. Goat, Gaspacho, asparagus and Migas, breadcrumbs in garlic, were flying about as though they'd forgotten the sun also rises. The decidedly amused debate didn't stop there. Pepe, and quite such a toothless charmer is yet to prop up a local bar, suddenly disappeared and began to beat up a blameless vat of olive oil, with a livid looking egg yoke.

In the shake of a donkey's tail, bowls of Gaspachuelo had

appeared, a true peasant dish. It's really oily egg with bits of bread, floating about in mayonnaise-flavoured hot water. At two in the morning it was a shock to the central nervous system, and I'm still not sure who the yoke was really on, me or them. But they seemed to enjoy it and I'd savoured a real flavour of the countryside. There are truer wonders in Arxarquía to be sent back to civilisation, but at least the Mayonnaise was home grown. And, for now anyway, when the sun sets here over ribbons of pink cloud, and the moon hangs off the stars like a paper cut-out, frankly the olives can get ... *estuffido*.

# Melissa Rossi

It's 9:oopm on a Saturday and in Plaza Mayor, Madrid's handsome, loggia-wrapped square, a crowd gathers around a young gypsy girl who is formidably stomping and twirling flamenco style in front of the pastel facades and umbrella-ed cafes. Several blocks away in the barrio La Latina, the tabernas - wine taverns - are in full swing, and the belly dancing will begin in a few hours at the Moroccan restaurant Imshala, near the Opera House. The Cuban National Ballet Company will soon be jete-ing, Cyrano de Bergerac will begin wooing Roxanne at Teatro España, Tchaikovsky will echo through the National Auditorium, experimental plays will mystify intellectuals in gardens, and the boisterous drag show will kick up at Gula Gula. Within an hour or two, restaurants from Basque to Russian, Argentinian to "aphrodisiacal" will start packing out, though there are probably tables now - since no respectable Madrileño would head out for dinner before 10, if then. The hot dance spots won't even get into full swing until 3 and they keep going till dawn.

Unless you're a hyperactive insomniac, you'll never fit Madrid's nightlife offerings into a week, much less a night. So let's take it easy and instead go for a tapeo - Spain's take on the pub crawl, but featuring those little plate o' snacks called tapas. Mostly a tourist offering in Barcelona - where most tapas bars are run by Basques - snacking is an important preoccupation here and locals take their tapas anytime from after breakfast until the early hours. And the

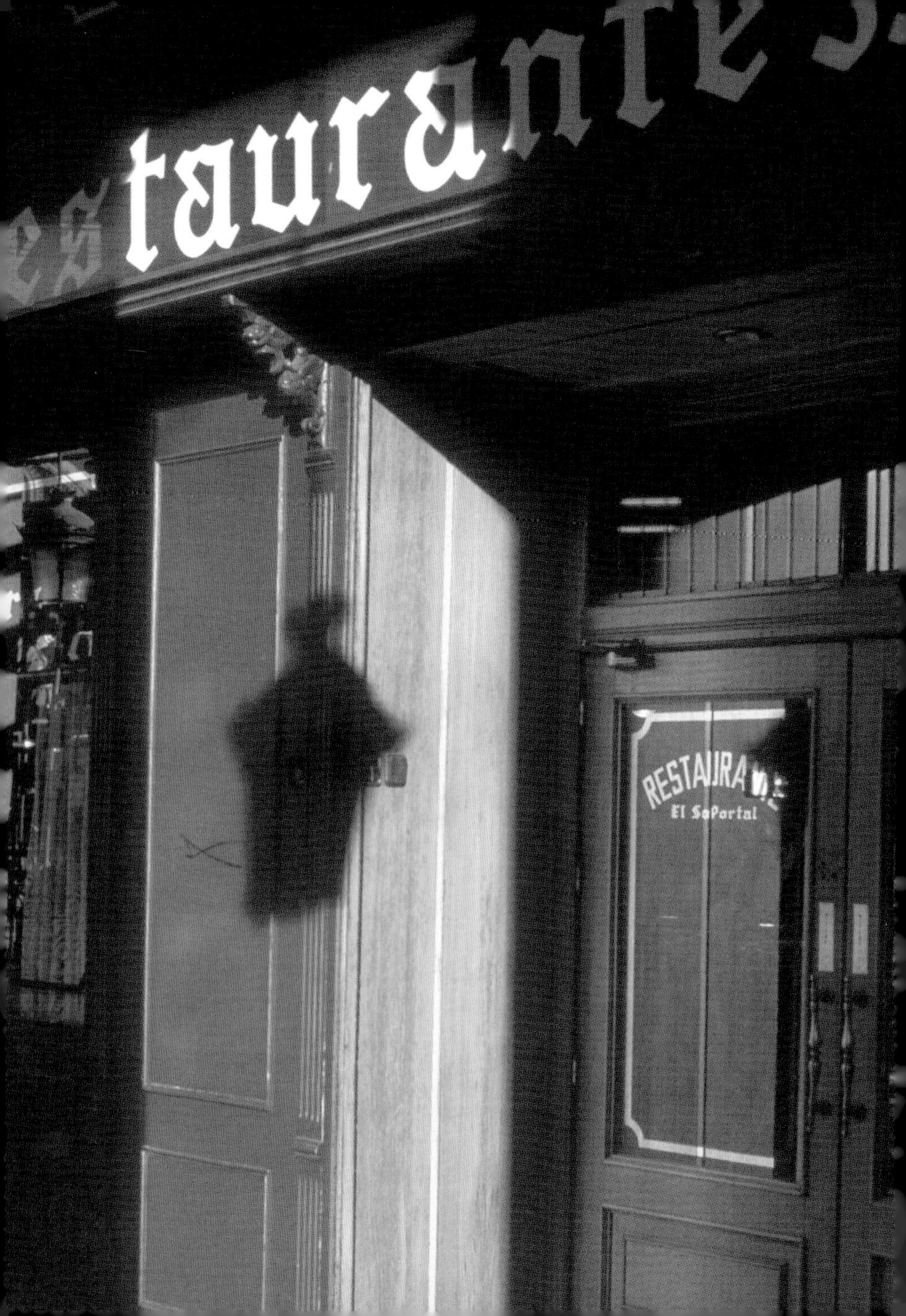
El SoPortal

center of Tapasland for my money lies near Plaza Santa Ana, a few blocks from Sol - the square that marks the exact center of Spain.

Designed with brick arches and miniature inset columns that resemble its Granada-based inspiration, Taberna Alhambra is a festive launching point. The tapas come on sturdy, oil-brushed bread, the two-room bar is filled with the laughter of young Madrilenyeos, and the waiters are very, very handsome. Try not to gawk at them too much as you order the tasty Cecina de Leon - ham dried in pungent mountain air - along with Viña Pomal served in oversized glasses. But don't get too comfy at the tables; around midnight they're put away and the Latin dancing begins. Besides, we've got to go - after all this is a tapeo.

Across hopping Santa Ana (lined with tourist-filled, overpriced joints) and a bit to the right is the tiny Plaza Angel, where we pass through the yellow and blue tiled exterior of España Cañi. Sparse compared to Alhambra, its bar is nevertheless cozy, and the garlic-laced Salmorejo - something like a thick gazpacho - goes great with a bone-dry fino sherry. You go ahead and order Sangria - but after watching them make it (with boxed wine, Orange Fanta and heaps of sugar) I'll pass. Before we leave, do buy a book of the owner's strange, sometimes heart-piercing poetry - some of which is written in English - which will come in handy the next time you want to say "the intrinsic caverns of emptiness" in Español. The book, 'Sutilezas de un Idiota', costs about the same as the sherry - a little over a dollar.

I know you want to head into Café Central next door to hear the killer jazz quartet blasting inside - but this is a tapeo and that's a café/bar. Instead let's head down sloping Calle Huelva, where you'll note gaily painted, wooden flamenco figures stand outside gazing out from apartment balconies. I don't know exactly why people decorate like this, but it makes sense since only a thin wood sculpture would feel comfortable perching on one of those narrow "verandas" that's about as deep as your foot.

Along the way there's a tree-shaded square outside Café Milano - but as always it's packed, and besides it's best for morning coffee; I'm not just saying that because yesterday morning a waiter there proclaimed me queen of the square. And no, we're not listening to any Celtic music in the Irish bars we pass along the way, and I'm not letting you drag me into one of the closet-sized discos either, even if they did just hand us a ticket for a free "chupito" or tiny shot of some super-sweet liqueur.

Instead we're heading one street over to Calle Moradin and the Taberna de Conspiradores.

Plastered with movie posters along tiled walls, this is perhaps Madrid's friendliest tapas joint, where the above-average quality wines are cheap, and there's unusual fare - from strong homemade cheese that is Spain's answer to Brie - to a crumbly dried bread dish, Migas Extremenas, that's a favorite of shepherds.

Hey, you're looking a bit tipsy. Don't worry, we haven't far to go; we'll just stumble next door to the Jazz Bar. Should we sit outside next to the recycling bins? Nah, let's go in to the plant filled bar and listen to jazz in the half-moon booths - ain't it romantic? One night they played Aretha Franklin for two hours and I was so happy I tipped the waiter $3 - as much as the two glasses of wine I'd consumed. (By the way - you don't have to tip in Spain, but a standard is 5 to 10 percent.) How about some zesty chorizo - fat-globuled Spanish pepperoni - or tortilla - the potato pie that's Spain's national dish? You go ahead and order one of the shaken cocktails, I'll go for a Cuarenta y Tres - an after-dinner drink that tastes of vanilla and 42 other unidentifiable ingredients.

A left at the recycling bin and we're on eye-catching Calle de Jesus, with blocks of tiled paintings and hopping cocktail lounges. The two most popular tapas bars sit on opposing corners: at Taberna de Delores crowds spill out with their drinks onto the sidewalk. At La Fabrica, they serve three fish plates with interesting names: marriage, divorce and orgy. The bartender assured me orgy was the best, asking me with a glint in his eyes, didn't I agree. I prefer divorce, I told him. Besides, all three plates include bacalao - and cod just kills the mood for me - but you dig right in. Oh and by the way, next door is El Rabano - where they serve a fantastic menu del dia that brings the locals in by the droves. I always get the chorizo-rich lentil soup, roasted chicken and potatoes, red wine and melon for dessert. Not bad for $7.

Okay, since you're holding your stomach, I gather you're tapa-ed out. But let's go have a drink down the street at the Palace Hotel, where we won't find a local who isn't part of the staff. The prices here are steep and you'll pay the equivalent of a three-course meal for tapas there - but sitting under the giant stained glass dome you can easily imagine what it was like a few decades ago when the place was teeming with spies - not the least of whom was Mata Hari.

What? You still have money to spare? Well, it's true tapeos are cheap, so let's get back to the high prices you're used to and check out the terrace at the Ritz Hotel. The band that plays Saturday is usually hokey - alternating from decent Latin hits to nauseating version "Feelings" that will have you choking back the laughter - but that doesn't stop the turistas from dancing and besides the garden setting is divine. And since you're buying, I'll take a Calvados, the French apple brandy that I've taken a shine to here in Spain. Yes, it costs twenty dollars for the drink, but hey it comes in a snifter the size of a goldfish bowl and the pours are extremely liberal, about half the bottle by my calculation.

What? You still want to go out more? You're right - it's only midnight on a Saturday, and this is Madrid where the nightlife won't stop until 8 in the morning, not long before the famous flea market opens up. Yes, you're right - I'm a wimp. So all the 70 year-olds out having a riot tell me when I hobble back home long before dawn. So, yawn, you're on your own. Don't forget to finish the night with donuts and hot chocolate. About the time you're stumbling to your hotel, I'll be coming out for coffee - as always finding that cafes on a Sunday typically don't open till noon. Now you understand why.

# Gastronomic Planning

## Recommended Reading

**The Wines of Spain**
by Graeme Chesters, Jim Watson. Survival Books Limitied.
ISBN: 1901130916

**To the Heart of Spain - Food and Wine Adventures beyond the Pyrenees**
by Ann and Larry Walker. Berkeley Hills. ISBN: 0965377407

**World Food - Spain**
by Richard Sterling. Lonely Planet Publications. ISBN: 1864500255. A very entertaining guide to Spanish cuisine.

**Michelin Hotel and Restaurant Guide - Spain and Portugal**
Michelin Guides. ISBN: 2061001823. Don't leave home without this one. A comprehensive list, with ratings, of restaurants in every city, town and village in Spain.

## General Web Resources

**filewine.es**
This is the one-stop site about Spanish wine. Tasting notes for a large selection of the country's best wines accompany vineyard directories, a run down on all the wine-producing regions, and an excellent glossary, with explanations of all Spanish wines and terminology.

**riojawine.com**
Everything you ever wanted to know about Spain's most famous wine. The official site of the La Rioja regulatory body includes history, news, a complete directory of vineyards, information on

wine types and ageing processes, and even provides yearly sales reports.

### allfromspain.com

This site basically exists to sell, and will deliver just about any Spanish product to anywhere in the world. It also includes, however, good information on regional cuisine, and a large selection of recipes to try out once your delivery arrives.

### spainforvisitors.com

An entertaining site that covers most things Spanish. The food and drink section has a good selection of links to interesting and curious sites on the internet. Includes a useful introduction to Spanish wines.

### tourspain.es

More great information from the Spanish Tourist Board, giving an overview of regional cooking and specialities, as well, of course, as a few well chosen words on wine.

## Travel Specialists

### Euro Adventures

This Spain based outfit offers a wide range of gastronomic tours and cooking courses. Imaginative routes include the 'Iberico Ham' route, which follows the 'Jamon' trail through Andalucia and Extremadura, the 'Olive Oils of Andalucia' route, and tours that focus on the Basque Country and its cuisine.
See euroadventures.net. Tel: +34 986 221399

### Culinary Adventures

A Spanish company set up by culinary professionals to meet the needs of the gastronomic traveller. Country wide tours cover the entire spectrum of Spanish cuisine, and include tours such as

'Northern Spain for Gastronomes', and 'Spanish Spices, the Saffron and Paprika route'. Also on offer are half-day cooking courses in Madrid, Barcelona, Catalonia, and San Sebastian. These are led by professional chefs, and end with a three course lunch. See atasteofspain.com; Tel: +34 91 531 64 89

### Inntravel

As part of the 'Cook around Europe' program, Inn Travel offer three-night cooking breaks in Catalonia. A local chef gives flexible tuition, based around the desires of the clients. See inntravel.co.uk; Tel: 01653 629000

### Avalon Tours

An English-American couple based in France run these tours to La Rioja, following a flexible itinerary to the region's best vineyards and wine villages. Includes a trip to medieval Laguardia, one of the most beautiful towns in Spain. See avalon-tours.com.

### Martin Randall Travel

For an intellectual approach to food tourism, Martin Randall's 'Gastronomies of Spain' tour, with accompanying lecturer, chases some of Spain's most traditional cuisine around some of its wildest countryside. Follow the Royal sheep trails, eat wood-roast lamb in Sepulveda, and visit a variety of relevant eateries and museums. See martinrandall.com; Tel: 020 8742 3355

## Exceptional Restauarants

**Arzak** in **San Sebastian**, is the above mentioned, so-called 'best restaurant in Spain'. An army of staff minister to you as you sink into your throne-like chair. The food has as many accolades as Michelin can throw at it, and isn't at all bad (Tel: 943 278 465). Try also **Rekondo**, on the way to Mount Igueldo, for a veritable feast on the tree-covered terrace (Tel: 943 212907).

If you're in the hill-top town of **Sepulveda** then you're in one of the best places in the world to eat lamb. Do so at any one of the restaurants that boasts 'Horno de lena', a wood burning oven.

When in Madrid, and feeling wealthy, head for **Zalacain**, the best restaurant in town. If you don't believe me, ask the King and Queen of Spain, who always reserve their favourite table to sample the restaurant's Basque cuisine (Tel: 91 5614840).

Just outside Madrid, in **El Escorial**, is **Charoles** (Tel: 91 890 5975), a carnivore's paradise with excellent local meats and a present when you leave: in summer it's a straw hat.

Finally a word on Parador hotels. Despite grandiose dining halls and exciting sounding menus, the Parador Hotel restaurants often serve up bland regional cooking, leaving you sorry not to have ventured out into the surrounding town in search of tapas. The following Paradors are a proven exception however, and are certainly worth eating in: **Jarandilla de la Vera**, **Trujillo**, and **Santiago de Compostella** (See parador.es).

# Island Spain

# Island Spain

There still exists in Spain's Balearic and Canary Islands the very essence of the Mediterranean idyll - secret turquoise coves, a timeless existence, olives and wine - though these days it's increasingly hard to pin down. Even when trying to avoid the hordes in summer, by heading to the 'other', 'untouched' side of an island, these days you're still likely to find tomato-red, beer-swilling Northern Europeans. The answer is either to abandon the beaches completely and head inland, as Anthony Sattin discovers below when he walks across Mallorca, or to come out of season. Hire a car in late autumn in Menorca, and those tiny coves, or 'calas', might just be all yours.

The Balearics long ago assumed the rigid identity of package-tourism paradise. Whilst each island tries to market its own separate identity - Menorca for families, Formentera for escapism - the beach towns and resorts are these days much of a muchness: packed, loud, and late. Having said that, each island still maintains it's owns specific charm. Ibiza, erstwhile hippy hang-out, is one of the clubbing centres of the world, and stunning, if that's your cup of tea. Formentera does have plenty of the small island/wild beach charm which it claims, though the fact that it is the smallest of the islands by no means guarantees that fewer people are coming here. Mallorca, despite the mass-market marauders, has a distinctly glamorous side, a favourite of Michael Douglas and his ilk, as well as being the setting for some super-luxury hotel resorts such as 'La Residencia'. Finally, Menorca, whose secret beaches can be ideal to reach by boat or 4x4, is becoming another top rambling location. Like all of the Balearics, it has a rich, and largely unspoilt, rural interior.

The Canaries, seven volcanic islands just off the north-west coast of Africa, are, despite their distance from the mainland, still proudly Spanish. Tenerife and Lanzarote were over-run long ago by sun-seeking tourists, though the wild, moon-like landscape around Tenerife's 3700m Mount Teide still merits a trip to the Island. If you travel to Lanzarote, Puerto del Carmen is one of the few locations to still maintain some true Spanish charm. The secret nowadays is to head to one of the smaller islands. El Hierro, the smallest of all and least visited, is split like many of the islands into two distinct regions. Whilst the south-west shore is a barren, arid landscape, much of the rest of the island is wooded, a haven of waterfalls and natural pools. La Palma, which falls away around the central 2400m volcanic peak, claims to be the greenest of all the Canaries, though it also possesses spectacular volcanic rock formations, and fossilised lava flows. La Gomera is perhaps the most beautiful of the smaller islands, a circular mass of deep, sub-tropical, terraced ravines that run from the central mountain down to black sand beaches and the sea. Much of the island has been designated National Park, and is, like so much of Spain, fast becoming a walker's paradise.

# Anthony Sattin

———

August in Mallorca, immigration officials in Palma were turning away foreigners arriving without hotel bookings. The island was full and in the coastal resorts there was talk of water shortages and tourist surcharges. But not for me the crowded beaches, the mobbed markets and sweaty disco bars of the package holiday. Instead, in darkness, at six thirty in the morning I was walking through Soller with Roger. There was a slight drizzle as we crossed the main square, passed the town's heavy old church and joined bleary-eyed delivery-men, train drivers and road sweepers for a kick-start coffee in the Café Central. The sky had brightened by the time we left and the first of the women out sweeping their doorsteps watched us surreptitiously as we headed for the mountains.

We were going to walk the pilgrims' path over the mountains to Lluc (pronounced Looch), Mallorca's sacred heart, the place of last resort for its people for more than five hundred years and home to the island's patron saint. Not that Roger and I were going for religious reasons. We were stressed-out Londoners in need of a break. And yet the trip did become something of a pilgrimage. Not a sacred one, but a search for solitude, for space to think and breathe and for a glimpse of old Mallorca.

The previous evening in Soller I had visited an elderly English lady. A long-time resident of the island, she had first arrived after the war, on a whim, having seen an advertisement for a house to rent.

"They assured me that the sun shone in December. I said 'marvellous', and came for the winter. And I have been here ever since." When she first crossed the mountains to Lluc, there was no road, just a track that wound through the valleys. "We went by motorcar, but I think it would have been more comfortable by donkey or even on foot." When I told her that we were going to walk, she went all dreamy on me. "Yes, and so you should. Only way to see the place."

On the outskirts of Soller, houses were tucked back among orchards of oranges and lemons, figs and nuts. A valley road led to Biniaraix, shut up and empty, a postcard-perfect Mediterranean village where every wooden door was surrounded by vines, each window tightly shuttered. We stopped briefly for water beneath the shade tree in the square and then went looking for a path into the mountains. We found it marked by a small, worn signpost on which was written, 'Lluc a pie', Lluc by foot, its narrow finger pointing towards the now-blue sky.

Everyone has a different idea of beauty. Some of us have several. One of mine is this: a stream running through a grove of ancient olive trees, on the side of a steep hill carpeted with grasses and wildflowers. We followed the path that ran beside the stream, wide enough for the two of us and neatly laid with stones by villagers who go up in numbers each winter to harvest olives. Some eleven hundred metres above us towered the Ofre, one of the peaks of the Serra de Tramuntana, a line of hills and mountains that runs up Mallorca's west coast from Andratx to Pollensa. We stared up towards the summit. That was where we intended to stop for lunch.

Good intentions we had, good preparation we had not, but although neither of us were in shape, our first steps were

49

made easier by excitement, expectation and novelty. And then we found our rhythm, a common, brisk pace metered out by the crunch of stones underfoot and the creak of the old leather straps on Roger's pack. Above the tree line the sun smacked and we sweated freely, pleased with this evidence of our exertions. They took their toll, though; the pace slowed, the jokes ran out and we stopped more often on the pretext of needing to drink water and marvel at the view of Soller, shrinking behind us like something out of Wonderland. During one of these rest breaks, a young Frenchman walked at great speed up the path, slowed for long enough to tell us he was going to the top and left with a "See you there." I think I caught a smirk on his face as his disappeared beyond the rocks.

Suitably humbled, we hurried on until stopped by iron gates and a sign warning us that this was 'private property' and to 'beware bulls'. As we were swapping cock and bull stories in front of the gates, the man came running back down. This time he stopped for long enough to tell us that he was on holiday, that he liked to run to the top of the mountain each morning and that when he got to the bottom he was going to have his breakfast. He had never faced the bulls and he advised us not to try it. Instead, he directed us around the finca of L'Ofre, a large stone farmhouse where an elderly man was tilling his soil with an old gnarled rake, a sight that would have been familiar to the elderly lady in Soller.

At the pass beneath L'Ofre, the country opened out. Behind us was the rock-strewn ridge, up above the old man's finca. Ahead was the valley that led down to Lake Cuber. Think of distant landscapes of the Lake District, the lake down below, jagged peaks all around lit by shifting light. Without anything human to give a sense of proportion, there seemed something prehistoric about the view. At a copse of fir trees, we dropped our packs, hung our T-shirts to dry in the sun and ate a lunch of bread, cheese, ham and peaches.

Roger, constantly active, was dismayed to hear we would be staying for three or four hours to avoid the midday heat, but I settled down to sleep beneath oozing pines, on a bed of wild sage and rosemary. The birds that had sung so sweetly all morning fell silent in the heat, only the cicadas continued their persistent trills. First Roger pulled a book out of his bag. A little later, turning over, I noticed he was rebuilding a cairn to mark the path. Later still, he had whittled down a couple of sticks and bound them together.

"I've made a crucifix for the top of the cairn," he explained, calmer than I had ever seen him, adding a sprig of rosemary to his work, "so other people will be reminded they're on the pilgrims' trail."

We walked all afternoon, around the lake and then in the shade of holm oaks, their canopy of branches hanging low and thick, the leaves of years past turned to gentle mulch beneath our boots. We didn't see another person, nor any reminders of the other Mallorca down below. Instead we shed more of London with each step, with every clean, dry breath, and revelled in the fact that a place of such beauty and solitude could exist so close to the resorts.

The first house we saw that afternoon was Tossals Verds, a large, high-level farmhouse renovated by the government to provide accommodation for hikers. I don't know whether it was because he hadn't seen any visitors for a while - we had the place to ourselves that night - or whether there was something desperate about the way we scurried down the hill, but the keeper of the hostel looked wary. Our enthusiasm for the place and for the garden he was cultivating helped calm him down and while we drank cold beers and took colder showers, he prepared a dinner of grilled meat, rough bread and homegrown vegetables. We ate on the terrace, the hostel keeper bringing another jug of wine and then leaving for the night. Before the effects of seven and a half hours of walking caught up with us, we did what people from cities tend to do when they find themselves in such a place: we tested out the idea of living up there, away from the crowds and pollution and noise and hassle. We fantasised about ways of spending our time, until the last of the sun caught the summit of a flat-topped hill and the fertile plain below it. Birds of prey hovered over the valleys, searching for hares and small foxes. A stroke of mist covered the land as darkness fell.

We were hoping to wake soon after daybreak, but what with the tiredness, the wine and the absolute silence of the place, it was 7.15am before I was shaken by a jolly Roger. "Morning, Pilgrim." The guardian who had cooked our dinner was nowhere to be found, so for breakfast we picked over the remains of dinner, left some money under the empty wine jug and climbed away from the house into the cool, damp blanket of oak forest.

The jutting peak of Massanella, 1349m high, the second highest on the island, stood between us and the monastery at Lluc. We were walking over loose stones, the day not too hot, our thoughts clear and easy, and making good time until we were stopped by a glade that was too idyllic to pass. At the heart of the clearing, beneath a massive oak, shaggy with lichen, there was a water source covered by an arched stone roof. Inside the font there was an inscription, 1748, which suggested that for at least two and a half centuries, pilgrims heading for Lluc had stopped to refresh themselves here.

We had planned on doing the same, but the source was

dry, which reminded me of the warnings given to visitors about the possibility of drought. Valerie Crespi-Green, one of the most experienced guides on the island, had explained that the real challenge to walking in Mallorca in August was making water supplies last. Unable to refill our bottles at the Font and coming now out of the tree shade and onto the exposed slopes of Massanella, I understood her concern. We had a long scramble ahead of us up over scree and rocks and around patchy clumps of maquis and pampas grasses, under a sun that had dried all but the hardiest of vegetation to dust and soon reduced us to a sweaty mess. In winter it's a different story, for the top is often covered with snow. It was a point brought home to us by the ruins of a case de neu, a snow house, where ice was stored in the days before fridges. Several more ruined cases lined the exposed northern side of the pass beneath Massanella.

We stopped to eat beside one of them. From that mountain-top lookout we could see the succession of valleys that ran down to our journey's end at Pollensa and the long plain that extended from there to the sea and the shimmering blue Bay of Alcudia on the horizon. After lunch, we hid from the sun beneath a protruding rock and slept for a couple of hours, surrounded by alpine plants and watched over by a circling black vulture. Lluc was still several hours walk down a rocky path through the Comafreda valley, with nothing but birdsong and the tinkling of sheep-bells to disturb our thoughts. As we got closer, the pilgrim feeling came over us again, although on the road into the monastery Roger burst into an old James Taylor song about women and beer. At Lluc we passed the bar and instead hurried into church to give thanks to the island's guardian saint. The atmosphere inside stopped us in our tracks. The air was rich with incense, the walls glowing with marble and gilt, the altar was backed with saints and angels while the dome was covered with portraits of the apostles. Impressed, we tried to imagine how it must have been for pilgrims coming over the mountains a couple of hundred years ago. Beneath the soaring roof stood a group of women in headscarves whispering their Ave Marias. Others knelt in the side chapel where the miracle-working image of the black Madonna and child held sway, wrapped in legend and devotionary prayers. Lluc has probably been a religious site since before the Romans, with the current complex begun by crusading Knights Templars in the 13th century.

Since then it has become the island's main place of pilgrimage and over the past few years, has also developed into one of Mallorca's main tourist attractions. We had arrived after the visitors had left, when a reflective peace was settling like the evening mist over the valley, the growing dusk and the deepening silence, broken only by tolling bells and hushed voices. That evening, in the monastery dining room, we had another reason to give thanks as we were served a feast that included the local speciality of roast kid and a thick red wine.

There is a prayer inscribed in the hallway at Lluc and on our way out, early the following morning, the cocks crowing, prayers already being said at the Virgin's shrine, Roger and I stopped to read it again:

*'Set out! You were born for the road.*
*Set out! You have a meeting to keep. Where?*
*With whom? You don't yet know.*
*Perhaps with yourself.'*

"Or perhaps," Roger added, a hand on my back, "with you, a hot beach and a cold beer."

The trail from Lluc to Pollensa is one of the oldest on the island, known to have been in use since the Crusaders established themselves in the hills. It provides a long, beautiful, downhill walk, first through pine woods and olive groves and then across richer farmland, the ground beneath our feet changing over the hours from rock and mud to tarmac and paving, the bare rock and trees gradually replaced by fields and then by houses, shops and people. Pollensa, real life, package tourism, crept up slowly on us and the shadow of London crowded behind. There was a moment, as we reached the centre of town, when we might have said what a good time we had had and how fortunate we had been to have found that place of peace and beauty and to have tested ourselves in it. But there was no need. Instead we settled into a back-street bar with some men of the town. When they heard where we had been, they made us welcome, in honour of Our Lady of Lluc.

## Recommended Reading

**Walking in Mallorca. June Parker**
Cicerone Press. ISBN: 1852842504

**Ibiza Insight Compact Guide**
Insight Guides. ISBN: 981234473X

**Lonely Planet: Canary Islands. Miles Roddis**
Lonely Planet Publications. ISBN: 1864503106

**The Mini Rough Guide to Tenerife & La Gomera. Christian Williams**
Rough Guides. ISBN: 1858286654

**The Rough Guide to Mallorca. Phil Lee**
Rough Guides. ISBN: 1858287030

**The Mini Rough Guide to Menorca. Phil Lee**
Rough Guides. ISBN: 1858287081

## General Information

**abcanarias.com**
Not only an invaluable accommodation resource, but also the usual range of useful tourist information, including sports and rural tourism, plus a great 'quick glance' section that provides a rapid low-down on the Islands' main highlights.

**abouttenerife.com**
Where to learn Spanish, go shopping, dance in the Carnival, eat,

and sleep in Tenerife. Also lots on the island's history, its exotic beaches, interesting trips, festivals, and even its legends.

### balearics.com
Events, news, cultural background, accommodation, web cams, maps, useful links, everything in fact that you could ever need to find out about the Balearic Islands.

### canary-islands.com
This site, produced by the Rural Tourism Canary Association, is dedicated to rural and nature tourism on the Canary Islands, focusing on national parks, walks, places of interest, hotels and accommodation, and all things ecological throughout the seven islands.

### holidaysuncovered.co.uk
Once again holidays-uncovered give us the chance to cheat the holiday companies of the chance to cheat us. Hard hitting consumer reviews of properties and resorts all over Island Spain.

### ibiza-spotlight.com
Whether you intend to travel to Ibiza or just move there for good, this site provides everything you'll need to know. Hotel guides, all the clubbing lowdown including DJ dates and nights listings, business opportunities, sight-seeing, even a section headed 'The best of Ibiza for the beautiful people', whoever they may be.

### mtn.co.uk/features/mallorca1-1.htm
The complete guide for those of us that just have to go mountain climbing whilst on holiday in Mallorca.

## Specialist Travel Operators

### Alternative Mallorca

A small family run company with over twenty five years experience
in providing accommodation on the island. Search for your hotel,
farmhouse, villa or 'casita' using criteria such as peaceful location,
bird watching or beach nearby, and sea view.
alternativemallorca.com; Tel: 0870 754 4545

### Astbury Formentera

Over twenty years of experience in bringing clients to villas in various locations on this, the smallest of the Balearic islands.
formentera.co.uk; Tel: 01642 210163

### Bonaventure Specialist Selection

Simple hotel-based holidays in four and five star accommodation
on all of the Canary Islands. bonaventure-holidays.com;
Tel: 020 8780 1311

### Lanzarote Leisure

This company promises superior villa and apartment holidays on
the long standing favourites of Lanzarote, Fuerteventura and
Tenerife. Most properties come with private pool and are close to
the beach. lanzarote-leisure.co.uk; Tel: 020 8449 7441

### Island Wandering

Island hopping holidays in the Canaries, with the possibility of specialist study tours (botany and geology for example), fly-drive holidays, and 'go as you please' accommodation only packages.
islandwandering.com; Tel: 01580 860733

### Ramblers Holidays

If you want to follow in the footsteps of Anthony Sattin (above),

Ramblers Holidays will guide you safely through the mountains of Mallorca. ramblersholidays.co.uk; Tel: 01707 339039

### Sensations Holidays
Ibiza is a popular gay and lesbian destination. Sensation holidays offer a wide range of gay friendly accommodation packages near the most popular gay areas on the Island.
sensationsholidays.com; Tel: 020 8902 7177

### Simply Travel
Island wandering holidays to both the Canaries and the Balearic Islands allow the combination of two or three islands within a single holiday. Includes La Gomera in its range of destinations.
simply-travel.com; Tel: 020 8541 2218

### Scott Dunn
Scott Dunn specialise in extremely up market hotels and villas with pools on the island of Mallorca. Many are set back from the coast with spectacular views onto mountain scenery.
scottdunn.com; Tel: 020 8682 5040

## Accommodation

### Owners Direct
Owners direct offer the chance to book directly with the owners of villas and apartments throughout the Balearic Islands.
ownersdirect.co.uk; Tel: 01372 722708

### International Chapters
A good selection of pleasant villas on each of the Balearics, particularly strong in Mallorca and Ibiza
villa-rentals.com; Tel: 020 7722 0722

**Villa Retreats**
Villas primarily in Mallorca and Menorca. Includes a selection of 'Exclusive Retreats' such as The Folly, a vast villa in Mallorca with indoor pool, Jacuzzi, steam room and squash court.
villaretreats.com; Tel: 01625 586586

**Holiday-Rentals.com**
Includes 97 properties on the Canaries, most on Lanzarote, and particularly in Puerto del Carmen.
holiday-rentals.co.uk; Tel: 020 8743 5577

## Getting There

**British Midlands**: East Midlands airport to Palma Mallorca
**Iberia**: via Madrid to all the Balearic and Canary Islands
**British Airways**: Palma Mallorca, Tenerife, Lanzarote and Gran Canaria
**GB Airways**: Gran Canaria, Lanzarote, Palma de Mallorca and Tenerife
**EasyJet**: Palma Mallorca
**Go:** Palma Mallorca
For contact details see 'City Planning' above.

**Trasmediterranea Company**
Cadiz to Gran Canaria, Tenerife and La Palma.
Barcelona to Mallorca, Ibiza, Menorca.
Valencia to Mallorca, Ibiza, Menorca.
Denia to Formentera.
Find them at trasmediterranea.es

# Fiesta Spain

# Fiesta Spain

Spain is still a country mercifully free of petty rules and stifling regulations. If someone wants to run in front of a bull, wrestle a wild horse to the ground, hurl fireworks or rotten tomatoes at the neighbours, then so be it. If it's fiesta time, anything goes. More often than not, our most common response to the wild abandon of a fiesta in full flow is 'That would never be allowed at home', a sentiment never better expressed than during the pyrotechnic extravaganza of Las Fallas, as you'll read in the 'Letter from Valencia' below.

The fiesta calender really gets underway in Easter, 'Semana Santa', an ideal time to head south to see the elaborate religious processions. From then on, there isn't a fiesta-free day in Spain until late Autumn. You'll find festivals of strength in the Basque country, mock battles between Moors and Christians along the Mediterranean coast, human pyramid competitions in Catalonia, and indulgent, epicurean sherry Ferias throughout Andalucia. An excess of care-free goodwill, food and drink, and endless outdoor nights are common to them all.

The popularity of the bigger fiestas, particularly Pamplona's San Fermin, Las Fallas, and the April Fair in Seville, can make accommodation a big problem: for these you will need to book rooms up to a year in advance. It's often easiest to stay nearby and use public transport to drop in and out of festivities in short sharp bursts. Alternatively, seek out similar fiestas nearby: Easter in Cadiz or Arcos de la Frontera instead of Seville, Las Fallas celebrations in Gandia or Alicante instead of Valencia. The experience will be all the better for a lack of oppressive crowds.

Often the very best way to experience the Spanish Fiesta is to come across it by surprise. Ask the locals, check with the tourist offices, and keep your eyes open. In La Rioja a vineyard owner led me to the annual fiesta in a nearby hamlet besieged by fields of vines. It was February, we sat in warm sunshine sipping Rioja from plastic cups, as the locals danced in dizzying circles to the enthusiastic sounds of a young brass band. "You should have come yesterday, we've been going all night", they all told me, as they paused for a late lunch at four o'clock in the afternoon.

# Benjamin Curtis

────────

## LAS FALLAS

"In Valencia we are quieter, more tranquil than the people in Madrid" said the taxi driver who was taking me from the city centre to the beach. "Do you know Las Fallas?" he asked. I told him that indeed I did, and came down from the capital every year to enjoy the festivities. "Las Fallas", he added with a wicked look in his eye, "are tremendous!" Indeed they are, and about as far from quiet and tranquil as one could possibly hope to get.

This week-long gunpowder-fest, which ends in a blaze of city-wide fires on March the 19th every year, provides a poignant reminder of just why it's so wonderful to be British in Spain: "That would never be allowed at home" is a phrase that constantly springs to mind, and never more so than in Valencia throughout the middle of March. The Valencians, you see, have a terrible vice: their insatiable appetite for fire-works, explosions, and noise.

The city beach is a curious expanse of sand, twenty minutes from the centre and backed by some of the most dilapidated buildings on the east coast of Spain. It is utterly unappealing to lie on because the fine grey sand is whipped up by the slightest of winds and, besides, it isn't very nice to look at. I decided to walk along it instead, towards the distant apartment blocks that mark a point on the horizon where the inland mountains meet the sea.

I came across a roped off area the size of a football pitch; crowds were beginning to gather, two policemen were doing circuits of the perimeter on quad bikes (what a beat!), men and women in hard hats were wandering back and forth. Right in the middle, at the shore's edge, were some barrels dug into the sand. It turned out that there was to be a Mascleta at five o'clock: I'd never seen one at the beach!

At two minutes to five the crowd started to whistle; a sort of adrenalin haze rose in the heat and my heart beat unusually fast. At five on the dot, policemen and hard hats safely out of the way, the first rocket shot into the sky - Boom! - the enormous explosion echoed violently off some buildings far behind. The Mascleta had begun.

Up went a firework the size of a cardboard box, lumbering into the air before bursting into a host of smaller containers, that in turn ripped at the sky with bursts of ear splitting sound. Sometimes there were colours (Mascletas are really about sound) and at one point, much to everyone's delight, a Valencian flag sprang from a puff of smoke and parachuted gently into the sea. Some rockets produced a noise like static electricity, burning up in your ears, others scratched at the air like cats' claws on glass.

The orchestrator of these events is revered as an artist, the benign creator of a symphony of sound: it is in the final movement, the 'terremoto' or 'earthquake' stage, where he really shows what he's made of, hurling as much gunpowder as he can afford into the sky for the final few minutes. The beach trembled, the air in my lungs vibrated, even the sunlight seemed to shake: just when I thought like my eardrums were set to collapse, it ended.

After our 'composer' had done his lap of honour, to ripples of contented applause, I headed back to the centre on one of the new trams. Valencia is a city of opposites. Sitting on this ultra-modern version of one the oldest forms of public transport, you are taken through some decidedly rough-looking neighbourhoods: drugs thrive here but the police claim that they don't have the resources to stop them - too busy on those quad bikes perhaps. When these shanty suburbs disappear, allotments spring out of the ground, and for a while the city almost disappears.

Back in the centre the contrast continues. Frighteningly dilapidated buildings in various states of disintegration lie just around the corner from the smart facades of the Plaza del Ayuntamiento, Valencia's main square. This is the site of the biggest Mascletas in town - the first few Sundays of March, and every day for a week up to the 19th, see upwards of ten thousand people gathering at two o'clock to have their senses shaken to pieces. Each display typically lasts ten to fifteen minutes and the final 'terremoto' is so violent that one cannot help but be amazed that the majority of the plaza's buildings are still standing at all.

There is of course a history of incidents associated with Las Fallas and its Mascletas. Last year one of the rockets, effectively a grenade on a stick, failed to take off properly and fell into the crowd. It exploded amongst a trapped sea of bodies and put twenty-four people in hospital, some with wounds through to the bone. Imagine that happening in any other west European country: it would surely be the end of 'Mascletas'.

But not in Valencia, nor anywhere in Spain, are such considerations allowed to come before the pursuit of public pleasure. Back in the sixteenth century Filipe II refused to ban bull runs at public fiestas; despite his own dislike for the affairs, endless accidents and pressure from his ministers, he realized that his subjects were too fond of these events, and that it would therefore be unfair to put a stop to them.

This attitude is just as prevalent today as it was then. There is a notable lack of petty bureaucracy or restrictive regulations: if people want to be stupid, to put themselves at risk, then let them face the consequences. But it's nearly two years since they were forced to stop the annual live goat-drop from a church tower in one Aragonese village; and another town in Galicia was warned that its autumnal raft races might have to stop after a spate of drunken drownings. Can all this lunacy continue in these times of pan-euro morality? The evidence suggests that it can.

During my first 'Las Fallas' I attended a memorable burning on the last day of the fiesta. 'Falla' is the name given to the satirical wooden and papier-maché statues, some up to twenty metres high, which Valencian craftsmen spend twelve months of the year planning and building - Mascletas aside, this is what the fiesta is all about. At midnight on the 19th, having been on display for a week in plazas all over the city, these things are razed to the ground. By chance I'd found myself in front of the year's top prize winner; this one would be going up last.

A barrier had been erected at a safe distance, so we leaned on it and watched preparations get underway; a crowd built up behind. Strings and strings of bangers were looped over the structure, which depicted a scene from a fairy tale. Larger explosives were pushed through holes that had been knocked in its side, firemen turned up and started to spray nearby walls in an uncharacteristic display of common sense.

Bottles of kerosene were fetched and everything was dowsed liberally, then to my absolute horror, as a young lady was about to set the thing alight by firing a rocket along a string from an overlooking balcony, all the barriers were removed! If the crowd pushed forward we'd be incinerated -

the flames rose, explosions cracked left right and centre, the wind shifted in our direction, the heat was getting unbearable, this was madness! The firemen turned the hoses on us, everyone cheered, and the falla disappeared in a fiery shroud.

What misadventure, what irresponsibility (this would never be allowed...) - whatever happened to 'following the Fireworks Code'? But what fun - irrepressible vitality surges through it all. While the happiness of the masses still counts for something in Spain, questionably sane traditions will never be quashed for 'what-ifs' and 'maybes'. And long may that continue, for without 'Las Fallas', Valencia could not be Valencia, and without these small lunacies, Spain would no longer be Spain.

# Christopher Somerville

---

L'Encamisa

To beguile a three-hour car journey from Madrid to the province of Estremadura on a foggy winter's night, take a couple of Essex lads. Stir well, sit back, and wait for the tall stories.

In company with a couple of chums from Canvey Island, rock band manager Chris Fenwick and his "honorary uncle" Jim Sullivan, I am heading out of the Spanish capital in dirty weather. We are making for the Estremaduran village of Navalvillar de Pela, where one of Spain's most extraordinary and colourful fiestas, the Encamisa, is gearing up for its culmination on 16 January, two days from now. Chris's stock of yarns of life on the road with R&B legends Dr Feelgood has temporarily dried up, and I am nodding off in the back seat. So Uncle Jim takes up watchman duties and keeps us awake with technicolour tales of his adventurous younger life on and off Canvey as a circus and fairground jack-of-all-trades.

It is Frank Canada, manager of the Oysterfleet Hotel on Canvey Island, who has persuaded the three of us to visit his native village of Navalvillar to experience the Encamisa. "Hundreds of horses," he has told us, "hundreds of bonfires, maybe 30,000 people. A lot of hard riding and wine drinking, you know. My dad will make sure you get a ride, don't worry."

Worrying is exactly what I am doing, though. I have kept a respectful distance from all horses since being deposited on the ground by a nasty brute of a pony at the age of six. I can sooner see myself dancing across Niagara Falls on a tightrope than riding a horse in the riotous Encamisa.

Nobody is sure for how many centuries Navalvillar has celebrated the wild cavalcade of the Encamisa. But everyone in the village knows the story of how the tradition began. It seems that a Moorish army was encamped, one 16th January - maybe as long ago as the 11th century, maybe during the great Christian reconquests of the 13th century - on the hills overlooking Navalvillar de Pela. The villagers were in despair at the impending rape and slaughter. It seemed only natural to go to the church and ask St Anthony, whose Feast was due the following day, to get them off the hook. And their prayers were answered when inspiration descended on the supplicants. By the time they left the church they had thought up a way they might outwit the threatening Moors.

The villagers hurried to build smoky bonfires in the streets. Then, dressed in outsize white shirts and spiked headgear, they mounted every nag and donkey in the place and galloped round and round through the smoke, shrieking like banshees, banging drums and ringing bells. The watching Moors got the impression that the flickering white forms were a vast army of mounted ghosts, and withdrew without attacking Navalvillar. Olé, Viva San Anton! Long live St Anthony!

At three in the morning we arrive at the Canada family home in a back lane of Navalvillar de Pela. Frank's parents, Antonio and Petra, have long since gone to bed. But their dutiful son, who has returned to his native village from Canvey Island a few days ago, is up to answer our knock and usher us inside. Navalvillar is a very traditional farming village, and many of its old houses are like that of the

Canadas; they turn a narrow blank face to the street, but lead inside through a spacious interior to a big cobbled double or triple courtyard concealed behind.

A kind of robber's cave of an alcove is festooned with loops of dark sausage and hanging sides of salted pork. Frank grills lengths of his mother's liver-rich chorizo and pours us his father's strong home-made wine. The wooden bench I am seated on is scored with deep cuts, legacy of many a pig-slaughtering in this yard. The frosty night air smells of woodsmoke, herbs, horse dung and roasting meat, the heavy basic smells of Spanish village life.

Uncle Jim pushes his well-shined shoes with their gold chains closer to the hot ashes. Chris in his thick blue businessman's overcoat sips his wine and winks at me. "Essex boys on the trot," he murmurs through the fire shadows. "Lovely!"

Next day, the eve of the Encamisa, we idle and spin stories at the zinc bar of our hotel on the outskirts of Navalvillar. Towards evening the streets and lanes are buzzing with subdued excitement as we thread our way up to Frank's house between knots of strolling villagers, gaggles of scooting kids and steadily swelling numbers of horses trotting, ambling or tied up to wall rings. The show is starting to come to town.

It's another frosty night, and we stamp our cold feet on the Canada doorstep. Frank's father, Antonio, hawk-nosed and with sharp deep-sunk eyes, leads us to the blanket-covered family table, beneath which a big dish of hot smouldering ashes throws out heat. We wrap the blanket around our legs to trap the warmth, and eat couscous. Then we step out to hit the bars of Navalvillar with Frank and his sister Maria Guadalupe.

In the early hours of the morning, doing something not too unadjacent to the samba on the dancefloor of the Centro Sociocultural, I am feeling pretty good. I invest 100 pesetas in raffle ticket no. 494, and find I have won the night's star prize, a horse to ride in the Encamisa. It looks as if Kismet is drawing a bead on me. After consultation with the Essex boys, I swap the nag for three Ponies - about 20,000 pesetas. It'll keep us all in beer and kebabs for the duration.

A couple of hours' sleep and we are assembling outside Navalvillar's olive oil plant, where horses of every shape, shade and nuance of temperament are being unloaded from horseboxes. The dealers, copers and gipsies who are renting them out - starting price, £120 - strike deals and slap palms with would-be riders in tonight's Encamisa. I sidle anxiously among the horses, half expecting a bite or kick. But Uncle Jim is in his element, running his hand expertly over flanks and legs, blowing into dilated nostrils and murmuring, "Hey, quiet now ... come on, you bloody old fool, be quiet." An Andalusian grey, which has been nervously jerking its head, stands calmly under his ministrations. It's a kind of magic.

"What do you look for in a horse?" I ask Uncle Jim. He weighs up the question, then pronounces crisply: "Four legs and a  -ing head, my son."

In mid-afternoon we join the crowd outside the parish church to witness the blessing of the animals. Hamsters in cages, pet rabbits, goldfish, magnificent stallions, cattle, cats and dogs - all receive a dousing with holy water, showered from an olive branch wielded by a brace of grinning priests.

At seven we assemble in the Canadas' courtyard. The family's three chosen horses are led clattering in. Antonio shapes leather straps into harnesses, while Petra fusses

Frank and Maria Guadalupe into their formal Encamisa riding gear - white shirts, scarlet neckerchiefs and cummerbunds, blue jeans, riding boots and beautiful hand-tooled leather chaps. Brother and sister look magnificent, transformed by the splendour of their get-up.

We three camp-followers, kitted out in white shirts and red kerchiefs, hardly dare speak to these two firelit immortals. We take ourselves off in search of the village square from which the riders are due to set out, but lose our way in the smoke of the bonfires. We are plied with wineskins, jostled into doorways, fed on honey cakes and bumped by innumerable horses.

I undergo a catharsis. Faced with horses by the dozen and score, horses so close I am spattered by their sweat and choke on their sweet breath, horses whose eyeballs roll inches from mine and whose ribs are pressed hard against my ribs - I can either faint away or learn to love them. I learn to love them, quick time. Even when a bunch of riders comes bursting out of dense bonfire smoke at a half gallop, and the alley we are in has no sheltering doorways to offer refuge, I somehow trust the big animals to barge past but not actually over me.

The riders, maybe 500 of them, circle the village until they are tired out. Many ride two or even three to a horse. Tots not yet old enough to walk are tucked in front of their fathers, eyes growing rounder and rounder as they bump through archways and alleys. "Viva San Anton Bendito - Long live the Blessed Saint Anthony!" yell the riders, leaning from their saddles with one hand outstretched as if delivering a blessing. "Viva San Anton!" shout back the crowds, passing up wineskins and cigarettes. Bonfires crackle and blaze on the street corners, draping heavy veils of smoke across

Navalvillar. Some riders make their mounts rear back on their hind legs, for dramatic effect; others try to jump the fires. Bands march and play, everyone yells, and underpinning all is the staccato, hollow clatter of shod hooves on cobbles and tarmac.

Maria Guadalupe reins up beside us - and beside herself, judging by the ecstatic bulge of her eyes. Chris Fenwick is boosted up behind her. "Christ ...!" I hear him gasp; then they are away, Chris's white-shirted figure jolting and bobbing. Suddenly it's my turn: Frank rides up, grinning fixedly, crazed with festival spirit. Hands grab my belt and throw me up behind him. We are off, before I have time to ask myself what the devil I think I'm doing.

Immediately the spirit of the Encamisa invades me. I relax my vice-like grip on Frank and lean outboard from the horse, shouting "Viva San Anton Bendito!" with the best of them. Faces blur below. We jolt, bump and bounce. I tilt a wineskin to my mouth - where has that come from? - and feel the wine course down my throat and spurt wildly over my neck and chest. Drums thump and hooves roar. The horse slips and stumbles, and I laugh like a crazy man, buoyed up to invulnerability. Maria Guadalupe suddenly materialises alongside, and now it is Uncle Jim grinning over her shoulder. They whirl away, swallowed by the smoke of the bonfires.

Midnight, or is it two in the morning? The striking clocks of Navalvillar seem uncertain. A muted roar of revelry seethes in the distance like waves on shingle. We are walking between fields on the edge of the village under a starry sky, leading the sweaty Canada horses back to the stable.

Between the blurred madness of the Encamisa riding

that has just ended, and the imminent haziness of the bar and dancehall trawl that has not yet begun, here is one moment of crystal clarity: hawk-faced Antonio walking with his arm around Chris, the wintry twinkle of thousands of stars overhead, the hollow double clop of the hooves, and out of the cold and dark a gentle whickering as the horses that have been waiting all evening in the stable greet their home-coming companions.

# Christopher Somerville

Anyone foolish enough to get themselves lost driving a Madrid-registered car during morning rush hour in Barcelona will quickly get a pretty good idea of the self-assertive prickliness of the capital city of Catalunya. That applies in spades if you arrive in the city on 24 September, the culmination of the great September celebration of the Festa de la Mercè. The Festa is a wild knees-up and assertion of regional identity, for which the citizens rehearse enthusiastically late into the night in the street bars of Barcelona.

Any self-respecting Catalunyan, and especially a Barcelonian, knows full well that it is historic and prosperous Barcelona rather than upstart Madrid that is Spain's premier city. The Barcelonians, delighted on this Day of Days to express their superiority over a feeble driver from the rival city, hooted furiously and shook their fists as I wobble timidly along the crowded boulevards at 30 kph. Such was my introduction to the Festa de la Mercè. It was a great relief to pull out of the snarling traffic into a parking bay. I vowed not to touch the car again all week.

It was back in the 13th century that La Madonna de la Mercè, the Madonna of Largesse, appeared in a dream to local saint Pere Nolasc, bidding him to establish a religious order to succour Christians captured by Barbary pirates. In 1637 the Madonna saved Barcelona from a plague of locusts, and her status as patron saint of the city was assured for ever more.

The festival in her honour was a tame affair until a few

years ago. Under General Franco's regime it was limited to a couple of pallid processions. After the old dictator's death in 1975 (ending 35 years of repression of the language and customs of Catalunya) the Festa de la Mercè took off in a big way, a popular explosion of delight in new-found freedom.

Whatever was big, bright and Catalunyan - carnival giants, human towers, traditional music and dancing - was borrowed from the various local festivals of the region and hitched on to Barcelona's big day. Since then the festival has swollen into a huge multi-day affair, and has grown far away from its original religious and very localised roots. Not that the participants or spectators care. The Festa de la Mercè is not some synthetic revival dreamed up by the tourist board; it is a joyful, rowdy expression of Catalunyan, and especially Barcelonian, identity.

Barcelona is a great walking town. But not for the sake of fresh air, and certainly not for the solitude on Festa day. The fumes of the city stung harshly in my nose as I inched towards the Ramblas, one among twenty thousand making for Barcelona's famous promenade. At the top of the Ramblas I pressed a brass tap and took a drink from the fountain of Les Canalettes. Strangers who do this, legend says, are sure to return to Barcelona. Then I sauntered along the thoroughfare, nibbling a pastry bought from a street vendor and listening to the sweet singing of finches, sad captives from the countryside hung up in little wicker cages to give passers-by a frisson of rurality.

In the cool vaulted hall of the Palau de la Virreina, athletic young men and women were inserting themselves into the papier-maché bodies of mythical beasts and monsters. Giants loomed 15 feet tall, experimentally spinning round with a swirl of skirts. Their attendants were

77

getting ready, too, winding themselves into ten-foot sashes, nervously puffing at cigarettes, checking their costumes. Half an hour to the off, and the pre-parade jitters were well under way.

I left the paraders to their nail-chewing and fag-puffing, and went off to shuffle with the crowds through the narrow medieval streets of the Ciutat Vella, the old city of Barcelona. Everyone moved at a snail's pace. I got my elbow in someone's ribs, and someone else got theirs in mine. But eventually we all squeezed out beside the basilica in the jam-packed Plaça de la Mercè.

The crowd seethed murmurously as a human tower of young men standing on each others' shoulders began to build itself in front of the basilica's open door. "You have never seen this before?" enquired the man whose heels were digging into my toes. "This is speciality of Catalunya. Nine peoples high is the highest tower that has been made. But maybe 10 peoples high today, eh?"

This human tower was never going to be a record-breaker. At five peoples high it was already quivering like a multi-storey wedding cake made of jelly. A young boy shinned up the outside of the tower like a monkey. At the summit he pointed dramatically towards the basilica door. Out came the Mayor of Barcelona. "Ladies and gentleman, I declare this Festa well and truly open," was the gist of his flowery speech in good broad Catalan. Clapping and cheering echoed round the square. Now things could get going.

*Els Gegants del Pi*
*Ara ballen, ara ballen;*
*Els Gegants del Pi*
*Ara ballen pel cami.*

*'The Giants of the Pine,*
*Now they dance, now they dance,*
*The Giants of the Pine,*
*Now they dance on the road.'*

So sang the children. The successor of the original Pine grows outside the church of Santa Maria del Pi. In the square, middle-aged men and women had piled their handbags and shopping baskets and were circling round them in the sardana, the gentle Catalan national dance. Rough-edged music came from the gralla, a wind instrument with the hoarse tone of a bagpipe chanter.

There were grallas aplenty in the Plaça St Jaume, where another sardine-squashed crowd roared and gasped as more human towers arose: human castles, in fact, buttressed round the base with a dozen stalwarts. Young men in white shirts and red sashes grasped each other round the shoulders to form a ring fifteen feet across. Others climbed vigorously on their shoulders to make the next storey. More castle-builders swarmed upwards on the backs and knees of their supporting colleagues, until the structures swayed 30 or 40 feet in the air. From the top of the tallest - eight peoples high, this one - a little girl swarmed up a rope and in among the dignitaries on the balcony of the City Hall, to the huge delight of the crowd.

Time for a breather. I nibbled tapas of monkfish and pickled peppers at the zinc counter of a bar, and drifted on: first down to the revamped waterfront where futuristic music harried the multitudes across walkways over the water, then sideways out of the crowd stream into the cool, shaded stone box of the Plaça Sant Felip Neri. Under the acacia trees, pungent smoke drifted from the lumpy roll-up of a dreadlocked hopeless artist. Water splashed soporifically in a fountain. This was relaxation made manifest.

In the cool of the evening I made my way back to the Ramblas, and took up station among the buzzing crowds for the Giants' Parade. Thunderflash explosions from the direction of Plaça de Catalunya heralded the appearance of the grotesques.

First came the scarlet-jacketed Urban Guards, mounted on horses and blaring on brass instruments. Next it was the turn of the Beasts: a crowned eagle, a donkcy, a garland-munching lion, a dragon covered in red and yellow streamers. Then the Giants hove in view - twirling, prancing, sinister and captivating. Gralla and drum blazed out as they bore down on us, a pageant of the city's history: 20-ft tall Saracens and knights-at-arms, fishermen and politicians, Roman centurions and buxom Catalan lasses.

Trainer-clad feet pranced and spun under the Giants' flowing coats and skirts. The Barcelonians scooped up armfuls of coloured streamers from the roadway and flung them at the swollen, impassively staring fibreglass faces. And I scooped and flung with the best of them, a Catalunyan by adoption for the evening, lost entirely in the spirit of the Festa de la Mercè:

> 'The Giants of the City,
> Now they dance, now they dance,
> The Giants of the City,
> Now they dance on the roof ... '

## Recommended Reading

### Spain. The Rough Guide
Rough Guides. ISBN: 1858288703
Details of fiesta dates at the beginning of each regional section.

### Fiesta: The Sun Also Rises. Ernest Hemingway
Vintage. ISBN: 0099285037
Classic Hemingway. Practically what made Pamplona the town it is today.

## General Information

### tourspain.es
The Spanish Tourist Board web site gives a good run-down of what's happening where and when in its festivals section. Also a basic search facility to see what's going on region by region.

### aboutspain.net/spain/info.festivals.asp
Dates of a large number of fiestas, not only in the big towns but also the surrounding villages.

### whatsonwhen.com
What's On When give all the details you could ask for on every single Spanish Fiesta that they can get their hands on. With links to appropriate web sites and full date listings.

### fallas.com
Diary of events, history of Las Fallas in English, and everything else you could possibly need to know (in Spanish) about what is quite simply the very best fiesta in Spain.

## Fourteen Fiestas

Beyond those in the articles above, the following fourteen fiestas are worth hopping on a plane to Spain for:

### Feria de Abril, Seville

Seville's April Feria is the aristocrat amongst Spain's festivities. The locals dress up to the nines in flamboyant Sevillanas dresses and tight country suits, before parading back and forth in carriages and on horseback, then dancing the nights away in vast, sherry-filled marquees. Also Spain's most celebrated bullfighting festival. Starts a fortnight after Easter on a Saturday (i.e. April 16th 2002, April 29th 2003, April 27th 2004, April 12th 2005, April 25th 2006) See andalucia.com/festival/seville-feria.htm

### San Fermin, Pamplona

How great a debt of gratitude this small Pyrenean town owes to Ernest Hemingway is unclear. Certainly this isn't the only urban knees-up in Spain with bull running, parades and bullfights. It is, however, the only one that a famous American author wrote a book about. In any case it has become the biggest, most unrelenting and wildest party in Europe, drawing millions of revellers and fool-hardy bull runners from all over the world. Pamplona, Navarra. July 6th to 14th; See sanfermin.com

### Tomatina

Almost as well known as San Fermines is La Tomatina, when people come from far and wide to throw tonnes of over-ripe tomatoes at each other. After a few hours of crazed food-fighting, head back to Valencia for a dip in the sea. Bunol, Valencia, last Wednesday of August, between 11.00 a.m. and 1.00 pm. Further information: cyberspain.com/life/tomatina.htm

## Semana Santa

Tremendous religious processions all over Spain at Easter, particularly striking in Andalucia, Seville being the highlight. Bare-footed processions carry vast wooden floats through the streets, wearing elaborate costumes topped with unsettling, tall pointed hats. The week leading up to Easter Sunday. For further information see andalucia.com/festival/seville-semanasanta.htm

## Patios, Cordoba

It doesn't always have to be about doing crazy things to excess. In May every year the citizens of Cordoba fill their beautiful interior courtyards with flowers and plants, then open them up to the public and the judges. Cordoba, 5th to 15th May.
See patiosdecordoba.com (see 'Galeria de Imagenes')

## Malaga Feria

The kind of festivity that will have you so in awe of the Andalucian, flamencoesque, merry-making, outdoor, high-quality-of-life style that you may emigrate to Spain on the spot. Malaga, third week in August; See andalucia.com/festival/malaga-feria.htm

## Sanlucar Feria de la Manzanilla

A typical, Andalucian small-town sherry binge, with hundreds of thousands of bottles of local 'Manzanilla' being consumed in 24-hour, music-blasting, sevillanas-dancing mayhem. Come to see the extravagant polka-dot dresses alone. Similar ferias also take place in nearby Jerez and El Puerto de Santa Maria.
Sanlucar de Barrameda, Cadiz. Last week in May.
For precise dates check: aytosanlucar.org/acti.htm

## Las Cruces, Granada

The town is filled with flower strewn crosses, about which much dancing and feasting will occur. The lordly rural landowners come riding into town on magnificent horses, with their ladies, sitting sidesaddle, tucked up behind them. An ideal time to visit Granada. (May 3rd)

## Semana Grande, San Sebastian

If you like to see teams of mighty Basques striking out to sea in giant canoes, then this is the one for you. Otherwise come for the international fireworks competition held every night above beautiful la Concha bay. San Sebastian, second week of August. See paisvasco.com/donostia/activialli.htm

## Moors and Christians

All along the Mediterranean coast, mock battles rage, commemorating the expulsion of the Moors from Spain. There are magnificent costumes and parades, as well as the usual firecrackers and partying. Calpe is my choice, as it's warm and uncluttered at this time of year. Calpe, Valencia Province, 19th to 22nd October; See morosicristians.com/ingles.htm

## 'Castells' in Tarragona

This biannual competition may just be the most insane event in Spain. Teams from all over the region gather in Tarragona's bullring to compete in building the highest human towers. Feet on shoulders, these may reach up to ten levels high, are crowned by tiny children, and invariably collapse in heart-stopping crushes of limbs. Madness. Tarragona, Catalonia. Beginning October (check with local Tourist Board, tel: 977 233 415). See fut.es

## Galician Horse Fairs

Throughout the region in summer, brave young men gather up the wild horses that wander about the countryside for their annual haircut. A true struggle of man and beast in idyllic rural

surroundings. Candaoso, Viveiro, Galicia, first Sunday of July
For other places and dates, see: galinor.es

## Carnival in Cadiz

A week-long fancy dress extravaganza with the usual attendant
partying. The locals will tell you that no other event in Spain can
hold a torch to this one and, as street parties go, they may just be
right. Cadiz, week leading up to lent.
andalucia.com/festival/carnival-cadiz.htm

## Carnival in Santa Cruz, Tenerife

Then again, the residents of Santa Cruz may dispute that. This
one is second only to Rio's carnival, and ends on the beach with
the burial of a giant sardine, to herald, somehow, the beginning of
Lent. Santa Cruz, Tenerife, week leading up to lent.
Further information: carnavaltenerife.com

# Accommodation

As mentioned in the introduction, it is extremely difficult to find
accommodation during the famous fiestas, especially in the
cheaper, hostel style places, for which you may have to book a
year ahead. It is always worth checking the larger hotels, however,
up to a couple of months in advance. The Hotel Turia in Valencia
(Tel: (0034) 96 347 0000), for example, is a reasonably priced,
four star establishment that tends to have rooms available for a
minimum of three days during Las Fallas, if you book in January
or early February.

THINGS TO DO 'BEFORE YOU DIE' No. 384

*Mountain Peaks*
"Witness mountain peaks emerging like islands from a sea of cloud. I've seen this a handful of times from the ground (aerial views don't count); most memorably from a snowy ridge in the Sierra Nevada, south of Granada." *Lee Marshall*

# Costas Spain

# Costas Spain

With the development of package tourism in the 1960s, and its subsequent explosion in the 70s, the sunny Mediterranean 'Costas' of Spain changed beyond recognition. Whilst some parts remain relatively unscathed, long stretches, the Costa del Sol and the Costa Brava in particular, were mercilessly developed, cashing in on the tourist boom when Spain's economy most needed a lift. Developed, however, does not necessarily mean ruined. You may not want to stay in a beach-front, concrete-monstrosity appart-hotel, but the rise in the villa and private house market means that beautiful, secluded accommodation in the hills behind may well appeal instead. Interestingly though, Benidorm, almost as high-rise and tightly packed as New York's Manhattan, is just as popular as ever, and particularly among the Spanish.

Beginning in the province of Huelva, at the southern border with Portugal, is the Costa de la Luz. Cool water from the Atlantic and large areas of protected land have helped to keep this stretch largely unspoilt and free of mass-tourism atrocities. Between Portugal and Cadiz you'll find wild, sandy beaches, with isolated pockets of uninteresting development, attracting almost entirely Spanish crowds. The inland town of

El Rocio makes an interesting base to explore both the coast and the fringes of the Donana national park, a bird-watcher's paradise. Far more interesting, however, is the run of sandy beaches between Cadiz and Tarifa, as outlined in the article below.

Heading east, the landscape changes dramatically beyond Gibraltar, with the start of the Costa del Sol. Whilst Marbella is all glam, a favourite Hollywood hang-out, things go quickly downhill between there and Malaga. If you are fond of tower blocks and the worst ex-pat excesses - English Pubs, German beer, satellite sports and cheap Chinese restaurants - then this is the place, especially Torremolinos. If you must come here, go for a villa in the hills, where you can view it all from afar. Beyond Malaga, things calm down considerably. Much of the Costa de Almeria, bordering the province of the same name, is wild and desolate. The Cabo de Gata national park still has a number of moonscape beaches, especially around San Jose, whose difficult access should ensure that they remain unspoilt.

The Costa Blanca, below Valencia, is a real mixed bag. On the one hand you have the unique spectacle of Benidorm, on the other the peaceful resorts of Calpe, Javea and Altea, caught between orange groves and a warm sea. Calpe is particularly striking, sheltered beneath a mountainous out-crop of rock, still warm enough to swim in October, a place to hire a villa decked out in bougainvillaea and jasmine. Alicante is great fun, somewhere for a weekend of beach, tapas and discos, free from most of the tourists, who tend to fly in and head on elsewhere.

Above Valencia the Costa Azahar has some nice towns with good beaches, Peniscola and Vinaros for instance, but the package tourism element soon takes over again when you reach the Costa Dorada below Barcelona. Sitges is famously outrageous and has a swinging gay scene, whilst Salou, despite a good beach, is English pub territory again. Finally, from Barcelona to the border with France, lies the Costa Brava. Once a rugged coast of secret coves, the southern half of this coast has been ravaged by inexcusable architectural blunders (Lloret de Mar is a case in point). Heading north, towards France, however, much of the coast has miraculously escaped. The place to stay here is the Parador at Aigua Blava, all the luxury you expect from the Parador chain of hotels, excellent sea views, and good access to the very Catalan towns of Gerona and Figueres, the latter being Dali's birthplace, and home to the fascinating Dali museum.

# Benjamin Curtis

### THE LAST WILDERNESS COAST

Many years ago BBC Radio 4 produced a series called 'the off-season', going to well known places when no one else would. Goa, for example, in monsoon season. The theme struck a chord, and I decided to travel out of season whenever possible, to see better what lies beneath the thin veneer of tourist crowds. So I was delighted to be heading to Spain's south-westerly Costa de la Luz in January, hoping to discover why this particular 'Costa' is so little known. I expected it to be overcast and cold, but at least everyone else would be kept away by post-Christmas economics and the new school term.

On the Tarifa road, south from Cadiz, crossing fluorescent green hillsides in twenty degree sunshine, past towering eucalyptus trees, like shaggy cumulo-nimbus clouds tethered against a swimming pool sky, it was obvious that the weather was anything but 'off'. Yellow flowers lined the highway, locals on mopeds rode past in t-shirts, and cattle gathered beneath bulbous pine trees and flailing palms. Spring, it seemed, had arrived early, or perhaps winter had simply never been.

At Los Caños de Meca, halfway between Cadiz and Tarifa, the beach, like the stringy village behind it, was deserted, the white sand and azure sea radiating tropical abandon. Something was wrong. January or not, it was all too glorious to find oneself alone. Heading a few minutes back to the Cabo de Trafalgar, where the famous battle was fought, I stopped suddenly, surprised to see a man float serenely past a sand-dune at head height. He was a kite surfer, one of many skimming back and forth across the bay, propelled by vast, multi-coloured kites that carried them high into the air when they changed direction. These aqua-aeronauts had gathered to make the most of the coast's most obvious natural resource: wind.

Down the coast at Tarifa, they've known about this wind for some time. Windmills line the hills behind, harnessing its energy, and windsurfers, lured by a constant force six, consider this to be Europe's best location. So forceful and unforgiving, in fact, is the breeze that sweeps through the town's narrow streets, that it is said to have driven a number of the residents to clinical insanity.

Tarifa's other essential element is Africa. Not 15 kilometres across the straits of Gibraltar, Tarifa is the closest point to Africa in Europe. It's an astonishing spectacle: the mountains of Morocco rise through the haze during the day, the lights of Tangier shimmer across the water at night. For those that arrive in Spain legally, via the daily Tangiers-Tarifa ferries, they may very well believe that this country is little different from the one they've left behind. Tarifa developed under Moorish rule in the eighth century, and the warren of tight, twisting streets in the souk-like old town has changed little since then.

For a growing tide of illegal immigrants, the proximity of these two land masses proves too much to resist. Night after night the Guardia Civil are stretched to the limit in their attempts to stop illegal crossings from Africa in small boats. On one particular night last summer, over a thousand people were rounded up along this stretch of coast. Many, however, are not so lucky, drowned in the strait's wild waters, their bodies washed ashore, then splashed across the front of

Spain's daily papers.

Ten minutes back up the coast lies a settlement of a very different nature. Baelo Claudia occupies one of the most impressive sites on the entire Spanish coast: the slow sandy curve of a four kilometre beach rising to a giant sprawling dune, the meadow-green valleys tumbling down from high rocky escarpments, dotted with tiny, fragrant purple flowers. These Romans knew a thing or two about location.

The remains of this town, uninhabited since the seventh century, constitute the most complete example of Roman life on the Iberian peninsular. Many of the Basilica's columns survive, as do parts of the forum, theatre, market and temples. The town was founded around the fishing and salt-preserving industry that sprang up at the water's edge, echoes of which can be found today in Bolonia, as the scattering of restaurants and hostels along the beach is now known. "Today's speciality is Sargo, a local fish. It all depends on what they bring me in the morning," says the waiter, jerking his head towards the wooden boats pulled up below the great dune.

So beautiful is Bolonia, populated largely by free-range chickens and foraging donkeys, that you wonder how it has been able to survive the ravages of large-scale tourism. The reason is two-fold. First, from midday, the beach is plagued by that same Tarifan wind. Lying by the sea in the afternoon is an experience akin to sand-blasting. Second, most of this land is now protected. Someone tried to put up an apart-hotel in the 1980s, a few kilometres up the coast at Zahara de los Atunes. They were stopped half-way, and recently the building's empty carcass was dynamited to the ground on national television. It sent out a clear message to other potential developers: the Costa de la Luz is not up for grabs.

Cadiz, at the head of this stretch, is the closest one comes to contemporary civilisation. Even here, however, there is a sense that it is fleeting, that the elements cannot be kept at bay. The old town follows a grid of low, cobbled streets, whose mysterious houses hide cool, plant-filled interior patios, built long ago on shipping and fish, all decaying, Lisbon-like, beneath the constant attack of salty sea-spray. Everyone wants to move into the new apartments on the road into town, and it won't be so very long, you feel, until Old Cadiz is another Baelo Claudia.

I leave with the feeling that there is always a touch of the off season on the Costa de la Luz, and that it is relatively unknown because it is unkind. No-one but the kite and windsurfers were there in January, and it's hard to imagine torturous crowds descending in summer. Three civilisations, after all, Roman, Moorish, and Modern, have struggled against that indomitable environment, yet still it remains a perfectly unspoiled and unkempt coastline of bright eucalyptus highways, fine sands, and furious, unrelenting winds.

## Recommended Reading

**Lonely Planet: Catalunya and the Costa Brava. Damien Simonis** Lonely Planet Publications. ISBN: 1864503157

**Costa Blanca Insight Pocket Guide**
Insight guides. ISBN: 9812345892

**AA Essential Costa Del Sol. Mona King**
AA Publishing. ISBN: 0749523719

## General Information

**andalucia.com/environment/protect/almeria.htm**
This section of the Andalucian Tourist Board's site tells you every-thing you need to know about the Costas de la Luz, del Sol and de Almeria. The site includes tourist information for all the main towns along the coast, accommodation listings, details on where to find protected national parks, and even tells you which are the nudist beaches in Almeria.

**Holidays Uncovered (costadelsol-uncovered.co.uk)**
'Check this site and never book a bad holiday again!' That's the promise backed up by thousands of no-nonsense consumer reviews of package holidays. Those that that have suffered drainage problems, bad food, terrible reps and hotels under construction, tell all. Links from here take you to similar reviews for all the Costas and islands.

**cb2000.net**
The Costa Blanca web site, featuring road and town maps, consulate contact details, weekly market times, town information, as well as jobs, villa sales and rentals, and weather updates.

**costabrava.com**

This Costa Brava site provides information on everything from museums to hotels, camp-sites and apartments to restaurants and golf courses. You can also find out what the weather is doing, and which discos to go for.

**comunidad-valenciana.com**

The Valencian Tourist Board site offers information on Benidorm, the Costa Azahar, the Costa Blanca and Valencia, including details of the best beaches, fiestas and cuisine.

## Specialist Travel Operators

**Mediterranean Dreams**

Mediterranean Dreams covers the Costa Brava, Del Sol, Blanca, Dorada, and de Almeria, and offers weekend breaks, luxury and standard package holidays, accommodation or flight only deals and a special 'build your own holiday' service.
See mediterranean-dreams.com; Tel: 0870 013 3366

**Cadogan Holidays**

If you really want to spoil yourself, try Cadogan, specialising in luxury four and five star deluxe hotels on the Costa del Sol, particularly around swish Marbella. See cadoganholidays.com; Tel: 023 808 28313

**Elysian Holidays**

Elysian have a big selection of villas and houses located around Javea on the Costa Blanca. Also villas throughout Andalucia, including two in Los Canos de Mecca on the Costa de la Luz. See elysianholidays.co.uk; Tel: 01580 766 599

**Spanish Harbour Holidays**

Concentrates on villas, apartments and hotels around Denia, Javea and Moraira on the Costa Blanca. Also offers similar

accommodation around the Cap de Begur in Catalonia.
See spanish-harbour.co.uk; Tel: 08700 270 507

### Rustic Blue

Rustic Blue claims to be the only specialist rural tourism agency actually based in Andalucia. As such they have come across a fine selection of hotels, holiday homes and private country estates along the Costa de la Luz (called here The Bay of Gibraltar), and throughout rural Andalucia. rusticblue.com; Tel: +34 958 763381

## Accommodation/Local Directories

### Vacation Villas

This Denia based, British run outfit offers a variety of hand picked villas and apartments on the Costa Blanca.
See vacationvillasspain.com; Tel: +34 96 6424505

### Villa Holiday Services

Based on the Costa Blanca, specialising in villas with private pools for up to fourteen people. Also offer beach-side apartments and town houses. See villaservers.com; Tel: +34 965 744 096

### Casa Spain

Fill out a simple form on-line and Casa Spain will show you a range of properties to suit your needs. If they cannot find your ideal holiday home, they will attempt to do so by putting your requirements into their 'Property wanted' section. Includes inland properties as well as all coastal locations. See casaspain.com

## Accommodation/UK Directories

### Costa Holidays

An on-line company dealing with all types of property rental (town houses, villas with pool, apartments, b&b etc) on the Costas del la Luz, Tropical, and del Sol. A particularly good selection of resorts around Malaga. See costaholidays.com

## Villa Click

A net based directory with a large number of villas and apartments on the Costa Blanca, del Sol and Azahar. An easy to use search facility lets you look for the accommodation you want, when you want it. See villaclick.com

## International Chapters

If their staffed, luxurious properties that overlook the sea on the Costa Blanca and Brava aren't good enough, then this company will even rent you a private island, just off the Costa Blanca. See villa-rentals.com; Tel: 020 7722 0722

## Villa World

Agents for privately owned villas in Moraira, Javea and Denia (Costa Blanca), Calonge (Costa Brava), Nerja/Frigiliana and Marbella (Costa del Sol). See villaworld.co.uk; Tel: 01223 506554

# Getting There

**Iberia:** to Malaga, Valencia, Barcelona and Alicante
**British Airways:** to Barcelona, Malaga and Alicante
**British Midlands:** from East Midlands airport to Alicante, Barcelona and Malaga
**Easy Jet**: to Malaga and Barcelona
**Go:** to Malaga and Barcelona and Alicante
**Monarch Crown Service:** to Alicante, Gibraltar and Malaga

For contact details of airlines see 'City Planning'. Monarch can be found at fly-crown.com.

# Activity Spain

# Activity Spain

Spain is the third largest country in Europe, the second most mountainous (after Switzerland), and boasts over 2000 beaches along 4000 km of coastline. The physical diversity of the countryside is immense: beyond the inscrutable frontier of the Pyrenees lie deep green valleys and fjords, dry rolling plains and wild national parks; in Almeria you'll even find a desert. Whether you're windsurfing in Tarifa, diving the Costa Blanca, riding or rafting in the Pyrenees, golfing on the Costa del Sol, or climbing one of nine peaks over 3300 m, the wealth of Spain's geography guarantees that you'll be in one of the finest locations in Europe to do so.

Two areas of particular note have opened up in recent years. Firstly the Alpujarras, a range of hills below Granada, squeezed between the Mediterranean and the Sierra Nevada mountains. This is exquisite walking country, warm and wild. Secondly, the Picos de Europa in Asturias, a mini mountain world hunched up on the Atlantic coast, with excellent trekking and climbing for all levels of expertise. If in doubt, however, plump for an activity holiday anywhere in Andalucia, where you may do practically anything, in perfect weather, at any time of the year.

With the majority of Spain's population now concen-

trated in a dozen or so big cities, the rise in demand for the activity holiday has helped to plug the economic gap for those that have stayed behind. Activity centres and tour operators with invaluable local knowledge have sprung up everywhere, and most activities can be arranged on arrival, usually via the local tourist board. Alternatively, as Philip Marsden discovers in the hills of Ronda, ex-pats with excellent knowledge of their clients' expectations can also provide fantastic itineraries, particularly for walking holidays. The planning section below lists a select variety of the myriad specialist operators now offering activity holidays in Spain, as well as some useful local outfits.

Those confident enough of their abilities may consider going it alone. Walking, cycling and climbing are catered for by an extensive range of maps and guides. These, however, must always be treated with a certain degree of latitude. Whilst walking the GR10 footpath across the Central Pyrenees, having lost ourselves repeatedly on maps that were anything but Ordnance Survey standard, I was desperate to rest up and re-supply at the remote campsite recommended by our guide-book. Unfortunate, then, that it had been closed for over a year.

# Philip Marsden

———

To the south-west of the town of Ronda are a number of flat-bottomed valleys which run unseen between pale limestone ridges. The valleys are high, suspended above the plains by steep-sided slopes which give no idea of what lies above them. Few people live in these high valleys and those who do, look at you from beneath brows which make deep shadows in the mountain sun.

There is really only one way to do justice to these remarkable uplands and that is to walk them. It is walking which must rank among the best in Europe. If the vagaries of local access do not put you off, then it is always possible to fly to Gibraltar, take a train up to Ronda, buy a goatskin flask, a lump of manchego cheese, a loaf of bread and some fruit, elicit a little local advice and a not-always reliable map and walk from village to village. Alternatively you can avoid all the uncertainty, all the gruff land-owners and the decision-making, and take one of two routes organised by Hugh Arbuthnott and his wife Jane.

Some years ago, the Arbuthnotts awoke after a "particularly good dinner" in London to find themselves in possession of a plot of land in southern Spain. The land had no property, nor any permission to build; they themselves knew neither the area nor the language. But, unwilling to go back on their caprice, they gathered their possessions and their two children and in Plymouth boarded a ship for Spain. There they cleared the brush, wrangled with the authorities, stretched their credit and built a house.

At the same time, they set about exploring the hills. Months of scouting and poring over old maps turned up the week-long routes they now offer. The routes are remote and just arduous enough to appreciate the stops when Pedro the muleteer will pull down a freezer bag of home-made lemonade and a bottle of fino. Then later on, with perhaps ten miles behind you, Paco and Pajarito will be there beneath the ilex trees with a couple of large cold boxes. You will lie on rugs and eat marinaded quail and drink gazpacho and cool Raimat wine.

Nights are spent in small villages or in hunting lodges where the walls are thick with stag-heads. On the Ronda walk, there are two nights beneath canvas at the Campamento de Castillejos. Shower-equipped and furnished with a pair of pine-framed beds, these are not so much tents as hotel rooms parachuted into the forest. Each is angled to view its own private slice of mountain, which in the evening is doused in sherry-coloured light. Ten hours later, between the flaps of the tent you can watch the first glow of the next day. The dawn chorus is a medley of warblers and shrikes, and, always from the same tree, the klu-klu-klu of a green woodpecker.

On day three or maybe four, high on the Llanos de Libar, Pedro called a halt beneath a walnut tree. One other man was there - Juan, who was clutching a blue plastic bag. He was sixty-seven years old and had known this path as a boy when under Franco he smuggled tobacco up from the coast. Another four hours walking would see him to the cafe where he would meet his brother and drink cognac and coffee. They would not talk much, he said, because his brother and he did not get on. He would give his brother the blue plastic bag.

"Goat manure. What he wanted was bat manure but he will have to have this."

After leaving the goat manure, Juan was going to walk back home. He didn't mind the walking at all; it was the walking and not the manure that was the real reason for his expedition.

"Walking up here makes me happy. After walking here I am always kind to my wife. Today I may even feel kind to my brother too."

# Jim Keeble

––––––

RIDING IN SPAIN

"Imagine you're having sex," shouts Mick.

I try not to think too deeply about this, given that my partner is a large brown horse. But I do start to rise and fall in time with the trotting. It's not exactly sex, more survival, but it is a lot more comfortable than before.

I love horse riding. The only problem is, I've not done it enough and I'm not as good as I'd like. Which is why I've decided to head to the Garrotxa region in the Spanish Pyrenees and ride in the hills for a week. Arriving at Can Jou, a restored 15th century farmhouse half an hour up a narrow track on the crest of an oak-clad ridge, I feel a little intimidated. Everyone else in the seven-person group seems to ride every weekend, and often during the week. Before breakfast.

On the first night I drink to calm my nerves, consuming a little more than my share of the excellent local red wine. I awake to mist pirouetting up the valley, and the naying of horses eager for my blood. Mick Peters comes into the breakfast room.

"We ride," he proclaims, as Genghis Khan must have done to the Mongol hordes.

Mick is an ex-farmer from the UK and he's been at Can Jou for eighteen years. He has the patience of a saint and looks a little like Butch Cassidy, which might explain why the women in the group seem to respond particularly well. Most of his guests are English, German and Dutch. The Spanish, he says, don't ride much. Riding is still considered an aristocratic pursuit in Spain, not for the 'hoi polloi'. We, in contrast, are highly 'hoi polloi'. There's me, Paul Reeder and Denise Clarke from Limehouse, East London, German nurse Carmen and her daughter Steffi, German physio Karin, and businessman Helmut.

We're due at the stables below the house at 10 am. And yes, the Germans are there first, but beyond this observation any nationalism is non-existent. In fact we're all getting on very well. They've kept quiet about soccer.

Each morning we have to prepare our steeds, check their hooves, talcum powder them, saddle them and harness them. My horse is called Pulida, which means 'clean', although with my amateur coat-brushing she rarely seems to be. Pulida, as Mick reassures me, is a gentle beast and seems highly sympathetic when I try to put the saddle on her the wrong way round. Before we set out Mick explains some important rules.

"If you drop something and we stop, that's a bottle of champagne. If you fall off, that's a bottle of champagne."

I ready myself to buy a case.

The countryside we ride into is gently spectacular. These ancient volcanic foothills are thickly wooded, laced with medieval villages and countless paths devoid of people. Garrotxa means 'land difficult to walk upon' but the horses, born and raised in the Pyrenees, are as sure-footed as a Riverdance line-up. Mick keeps us moving. "Trot!" and "Canter!" are words to loosen my sphincter. But our first day's ride is relatively easy - three hours in the saddle, taking in a ruined 13th century monastery where we eat oranges and gaze up at snow-tipped Pyrenean peaks.

The week is well planned - a full day's ride followed by a half day in the saddle and plenty of time to recover. I find sitting on horseback surprisingly relaxing, a time for happy contemplation, lulled by clopping hooves. On the longest day we ride to the medieval village of Besalú, where we tie our horses by the river and swagger into town like desperadoes to eat sandwiches. In all we spend seven hours in the saddle and cover 25 kilometers.

"Como esta tu culo?", asks Mick's Spanish wife Rosie on our return. How is your backside?

Surprisingly, it doesn't hurt. But my back does. And calves. And knees, and thighs and arms. My head feels fine though. Until I have another evening on Mick's wine. Flushed with equestrian success we sink several bottles and end up singing by the fire, a demonic Anglo-Germanic choir howling out Elvis Presley songs until the small hours. There is, I muse over yet another bottle of Vino Tinto, still hope for a united Europe.

Back in the saddle, my first ever gallop is the most exhilarating thing I've done since riding down two flights of stairs on a plastic tractor aged five. I even keep my eyes open.

On my last night I sit by the fire feeling more than a little pleased with myself. I begin to wonder if I might stay on to try the subsequent week-long trail ride from Can Jou, a trip which several members of the group are doing, where you travel on horseback from the hills, via small hotels, as far as the Mediterranean.

It can't be that difficult, I decide. After all, it's like having sex. For eight hours a day, every day, for six days.

Maybe next time.

# Christopher Somerville

EBRE DELTA

Over its 460-mile journey eastwards from the Atlantic mountains to the Mediterranean coast of Spain, the River Ebre collects an enormous amount of silt. For thousands of years the river has been discharging this alluvial cargo during its final push to the sea, forming a giant fan-shaped piece of land covering more than 120 square miles that juts out some fifteen miles from the coastline of Catalunya. On the map the Delta resembles an eastward paddling turtle, a big lagoon for its eye, the mouth of the Ebre its own upward-hooked mouth, and two blunt-tipped peninsulas to north and south straining landward like two hard-working flippers.

Entering the Delta on a sultry morning in early autumn, I found myself in a dead level world, its absolute flatness accentuated by the rugged profile of the Montsi mountain range as an inland backdrop. The most upstanding features of the Delta landscape were ancient towers, some square and others cylindrical, that rose against a cloudy sky. "These towers were built to watch for pirates," said Carmen Garrido, my guide and companion in the Delta, as she rolled down the car window and pointed out. "In medieval times Catalunya had big problem with pirates, and they came to land first on the Delta. The people would set the fire in the towers to say to everyone that these pirates are coming."

The Delta had been inhabited since the time of the Moorish conquest of Spain around 700 AD, but malaria - endemic in such low-lying coastal wetland - kept numbers of residents in the low hundreds for the next thousand years. A hardy handful of wild fowlers, reed-cutters and net fishermen was the only population able to tolerate life amid the swamps until canals began to be cut in the 19th century. Rice was the one crop that could thrive in the salt-sodden silt of the Delta. The newly drained and irrigated flatlands quickly became the rice bowl of Spain. Once malaria was eradicated, the population soared. Now 50,000 people live in the Delta, in villages and on smallholdings scattered widely through the rice fields. The rest of Catalunya considers them a race apart, web-footed, slippery as eels.

Carmen and I followed side roads that twisted between the rice paddies. Glinting spokes of waterlogged furrows wheeled between the recently harvested ridges. Canals and ditches hurried fresh water around and away from the fields. The river itself, backbone of the Delta, ribboned through paddies, villages and wet woods. This was a waterland, where hundreds of thousands of wildfowl were making a tremendous clamour on this September morning.

Everything I had heard about the Ebre Delta in early autumn had pushed my birdwatcher's buttons. About 90% of all the birds that come to Catalunya for the winter settle in the Delta. Well over half of all European bird species are present in this unobtrusive tongue of peninsular wetland. As for birds of passage, stopping off to feed and rest in the course of their long migratory flights up and down the world - the Delta is famous for them. With Carmen's knowledgeable prompting I was hoping to spot crake, stilt, marsh harrier, red-crested pochard, osprey, whiskered tern, collared pratincole; some of these shy stars, at any rate. Also, of course, the celebrity flamingoes, year-round residents of the salty lagoons of the Delta.

The Ebre Delta was declared a national nature reserve in 1983. It is a European Special Protection Zone for birds, and a Ramsar or wetland of international importance. Large parts of it are protected as 'natural park'. The Ebre Delta Natural Park authority has set up an eco-museum in the central Delta village of Deltebre - first port of call for any visitor who wants to understand and appreciate this unique place where a dozen delicately balanced ecosystems thrive side by side.

In the museum I got a vivid impression of an enormous variety of habitats in one small area. The River Ebre itself has a layer of fresh water running seaward at the surface, and below that a belt of salt water pushing in the opposite direction - two contrasting environments in the same place, supporting entirely different kinds of fish and plants within a few inches of each other. The dozen lagoons of the Delta, freshwater in spring and salty in winter, have been rescued from agrichemical and algal poisoning to become prime larders and nesting grounds for dozens of bird species.

The Delta contains saltmarshes where flamingoes and avocets feed, sand dunes and deserted beaches haunted by terns, knot and oystercatchers. There are 'ullals', freshwater wells fed by mountain springs, carpeted with waterlilies. And then there are the Delta's man-made environments, more or less successfully controlled to harmonise with nature: rice fields favoured by egrets, herons and lapwing; salt pans and mussel farms; orchards and vegetable fields around freshwater sources. Locals still hunt here, shooting duck, fishing for sea bass and mullet. The idea is to balance the whole life of the Delta, human and natural.

From Deltebre we made for Riumar to catch a cruise boat to the mouth of the Ebre. But first, serious business: lunch. "This place," promised Carmen, leading the way into the Restaurant L'Aube, "you will like it. Local people, they eat here ..." I did like it: paella as mother would have made it, had she known how, studded with locally caught shellfish and eaten on a cool verandah.

Afterwards, the river trip, chugging seaward past rickety jetties where small boys wielded fishing rods while their fathers smoked and yarned under the poplars. "Born on the Bayou," I found myself whistling. There were more anglers on the estuary sandspits, and fleets of pink flamingoes in marshy bays whose open mouths slowly passed by.

Carmen and I saw the flamingoes at closer range that evening, as we stole down a path beside El Canal Vell lagoon. We heard the birds groaning together like cross old men long before they came in sight. Their rod-thin scarlet legs trod the lagoon floor on the spot, like so many Michael Jackson moonwalkers. They were stirring buried invertebrates out of the sunken mud into the water where their big filtering beaks, sifting the shallows, could process the food.

Over the reedbeds sailed a pair of marsh harriers, big dark birds of prey only recently arrived from the north to spend the winter. Martins on passage to Africa went skimming low over the water. We saw them or their fellows at dusk as we walked the broad sands of the Fangar peninsula in the north of the Delta. This was a magical place, windswept and lonely, its flat wastes shimmering with mirage water in the last of the sunlight before ominous clouds shut the day down.

By dawn a towering electrical storm had built itself up and was bellowing and fizzing over the Delta. We drove from the village of St Jaume d'Enveja into a grey wall of rain split by intense lilac cracks of lightning. One bolt jagged deafeningly into a rice field twenty yards from the car, throwing up clouds of instantly boiled paddy water. Rail and moorhens scattered in panic across the flooded roads. It was a nerve-tingling start to the day, but by the time we were crossing the green and purple saltmarsh of the Erms de la Tancada the worst of the storm had flickered and rumbled away northwards.

A sandspit isthmus with a spine of rough road runs south for three miles from the underbelly of the Delta before broadening out into the Punta de la Banya, a big peninsular bulge of sand dunes, salt pans and miles of empty beach where we wandered all morning. Not a place of Blue Flag neatness: the narrow spit and the beaches were scattered with flotsam and driftwood. Unbeatable, though, for lung-scouring salt wind, seabirds wheeling and calling, green seas and a sense of desert island isolation.

On the mainland Delta again, Carmen directed me to L'Encanyissada lagoon where two thousand coot, just arrived in Catalunya for the winter, floated in a densely-packed mass. Among them I spotted Netta rufina, the rare red-crested pochard, and any number of great crested grebe ducking and diving.

I said goodbye to Carmen, and considered how to round off the afternoon. The decision didn't take long. Of all the splendours of the Delta, the wild isolation of the Punta de la Banya had stuck most seductively in my imagination.

Back on the saltings of the Erms de la Tancada I took my bird book and went strolling down the empty sandspit once more. Standing on a carpet of reed splinters on a deserted beach at nightfall I watched the last birds of the day through binoculars, a southward flight of crook-winged tern travelling towards Africa at a great rate, very high against a slate-grey sky.

# Activity Planning

## Recommended Reading

**The Pyrenees.The Rough Guide**
Rough Guides. ISBN: 1858287014

**Lonely Planet: Walking in Spain. Miles Roddis et al**
Lonely Planet Publications. ISBN: 0864425430

**Alpujarras Walking Guide. David Anthony Brawn, Rosamund Coreen Brawn** Discovery Walking Guides. ISBN: 1899554378

**Walks and Climbs in the Picos De Europa. Robin Walker**
Cicerone Press. ISBN: 1852840331

**Sunflower Guides**
Sunflower Guides produce a range of walking and landscape guides for the most important walking destinations on mainland and island Spain. sunflowerbooks.co.uk For example:
**Landscapes of Cataluña: Delta del Ebro and Puertos de Beceite** by Paul Jenner and Christine Smith (Sunflower Books - ISBN 1-85691-029-6)

## General Information

**andalucia.com/sports/home.htm**
Do you want to know where to play polo, green bowls or cricket in Andalucia? Also good on golf, adventure sports (climbing, caving, microlighting etc.), walking, angling, water sports and much more, all in Spain's most activity-friendly region.

**andalucia.co.uk/activities**
A directory of sporting activities and relevant tour operators, ranging from ballooning to hunting, windsurfing to snowboarding,

and scuba diving to photography holidays throughout Andalucia.

## pyrenees-pireneos.org
Don't set foot in the Pyrenees without checking here first. Lots of insider information on walking and hiking in the Pyrenees, including recommended books and maps, equipment advice and checklists, plus details of guides, guided treks and places to stay. Also puts together made-to-measure hiking trips throughout the region.

## spainforvisitors.com/sections/activities.htm
Good links section providing access to information on where to do, and how to do, a variety of sports and activities all over Spain.

## fell-walker.co.uk
One for the walkers, with general information on regions, recommended books and maps, and hints for good walks in the Canary Islands.

## Ebre Delta Activities
Birdwatching, fishing, bicycling, walking, river cruises, boating, swimming, surfboarding - for all information on solo or guided activities, hire of equipment etc, contact Deltaguìa, Av. Mallorca 61, 43877 Saint Jaume d'Enveja (tel/fax +34 977-47-80-24)

# Specialist Travel Operators

## Andalucian Adventures
Walking and painting holidays in the Alpujarras, the Subbetica Natural Park, and the stunning Sierra de Aracena Natural Park. Walking holidays are led by Brits with excellent local knowledge, while the painting holidays include expert tuition where necessary. See andalucian-adventures.co.uk; Tel: 01453 834137

## Biking Andalucia
This Spain based outfit offers guided tours in the Alpujarras and

Sierra de Nevada mountains south of Granada. Accommodation is in Cortijo farmhouses, and the company also caters for self-led groups. See bikingandalucia.com; Tel: +34 958 784 372

**Exodus**
Exodus, the long running adventure travel company, offer their new multi-activity programmes in Andalucia, combining, for example, mountain biking, ski mountaineering, canyoning and skiing in the Sierra Nevada. Also, trekking in Mallorca, walks everywhere, and winter snow-shoe holidays in the Pyrenees. See exodus.co.uk; Tel: 020 8675 5550

**Freewheel Holidays**
They promise gentle cycling holidays with as many downhill stretches as possible. Their Cantabria and Asturias tour averages around 25 miles per day, through mountainous and coastal regions, and includes accommodation in family run, off the beaten track hotels. See freewheelholidays.com; Tel: 01633 681997

**Golf In The Sun**
Golf in the sun offers golfing holidays at courses along the entire Spanish coast. Just choose your Costa and they will help you to select a centre. Tuition holidays to lower that handicap are available on the Costa del Sol. Holidays also available in Tenerife and Mallorca. See golfinthesun.co.uk; Tel: 01327 350394

**H F Holidays**
Excellent Independent walking itineraries in the Picos de Europa and the Alpujarras, plus guided tours in the Alpujarras, Ronda, Sierra Almijara, Mallorca and Tenerife.
See hfholidays.co.uk; Tel: 020 8905 9556

**Inntravel**
Inntravel provide fully organised activity holidays, including carefully chosen accommodation. There is cycling along the

Catalan coast, horse riding in the Alpujarras, the Sierra de Gredos (Castile), the Sierra de Guara (Aragon), Andalucia, and at Can Jou, as mentioned in the article above. Also, walking holidays practically everywhere, including Galicia, La Rioja, Asturias, and the wild, desert coast of Almeria.
See inntravel.co.uk; Tel: 01653 629000

## Menorca Sailing Holidays
If you fancy sailing around the coast of Menorca, or at least learning to do so with qualified RYA instructors, then this group will organise everything, even a creche for the babies. Also good for windsurfing. See minorcasailing.co.uk; Tel: 020 8948 2106

## Planet Windsurf
Holidays in, plus a wealth of information about windsurfing conditions at, Tarifa, on the Costa de la Luz, one of Europe's most famous windsurfing destinations. Accommodation includes hotels with names such as 'Hurricane Hotel', and 'Hotel 100% Fun'.
See planetwindsurf.com; Tel: 01273 746 700

## Ramblers Holidays
With over 50 years' experience in guided walking holidays, Ramblers Holidays' routes include 'more energetic' walks in Mallorca, and 'challenging' walks in the Alpujarras.
See ramblersholidays.co.uk; Tel: 01707 339039

## Sports & Leisure Holidays
Holidays along the Costas del Sol and Blanca, and in the Canary Islands, offer tennis and golf with professional tuition, in an all-inclusive resort environment.
See tennisholidays.co.uk; Tel: 01794 500500

## Ski GB
Ex-pat Giles Birch works as a ski instructor in the Sierra Nevada. He is able to organise accommodation and skiing lessons, and his

site provides a wealth of information about getting to and skiing in the region. See sierranevada.co.uk

## The Walking Safari Company

This is the place to organise a walking holiday near Ronda with the Arbuthnotts, as written about by Philip Marsden. Tours include tented accommodation beneath the stars and expert knowledge, including from a local ornithologist, all whilst trekking through cork forests, olive groves, and along ancient mule trails.
See walkeurope.com; Tel: 01572 821330

## UK Golf del Sol

A Malaga based company specialising in golfing holidays along the Costa del Sol, making the most of the 36 18-Hole Championship Golf Courses in the region.
See ukgolfdelsol.com; Tel: (0034) 95 259 2364

# Accommodation of Interest

**La Manga Club** in Murcia has the last word in luxurious sports and activities facilities in Spain. Tucked up on the coast of Murcia, with accommodation from the five star Hyatt hotel to self-catering villas, the resort offers three championship golf courses, a golf academy, 18 tennis courts, a range of water sports, a fitness centre, pools, and a soccer centre used by the English national football team. See lamangaclub.com

THINGS TO DO 'BEFORE YOU DIE' No. 1474

*Salamanca*
"Sit in the cathedral square as sunset performs its alchemy on the ornately figured stonework of the ancient colleges and churches of this university town, turning them a fiery copper." *Claire Gervat*

# Moorish Spain

# Moorish Spain

High amongst the cork forests of Andalucia's Sierra de Aracena, two hours north-west of Seville, sits the village of Almonaster la Real. The winding, white-washed streets, sweet with jasmine and bright with wild pea flowers, lead up to a lazy plaza where impossibly dark-skinned children run around the fountain. From here, one last street leads on up the hill, past the diminutive bull-ring, to the finest little mosque in Spain. The modest exterior hides rows of tell-tale tenth century horse-shoe arches. At the back, steps wind up inside the towering minaret from where, high up in a warm breeze, you can gaze across the silent green Sierra. Here is the essence of Moorish Spain, a work of striking architectural simplicity in a setting of outstanding natural beauty.

In the eighth century Muslim invaders blazing a path across North Africa crossed the Straits to Spain, liked what they found, and stayed. They brought with them the most evolved civilisation of the time, sweeping the dark cobwebs of middle age Christianity out from under them as they moved north. Only when they got as far as Asturias, where they were met with unconquerable resistance, did their domination of Spain come to a halt. From there they were eventually driven south again, finally to be ejected from the magnificent kingdom of Granada in the fifteenth century, seven hundred years after they had arrived.

Evidence of their legacy can be found all over the country: in Spain's culture and cuisine, above all in the architectural wonders found everywhere, and perhaps even in those impossible tans in Almonaster. The intricacies of Granada's Alhambra Palace, said to be the finest combination of gardens, light, water and stone on earth, should of course be seen above anything else. But what of Seville's Alcazar, Malaga's Alcazaba, or the magnificent Mudejar towers built by Moorish craftsmen in Teruel?

Foolish would be the traveller who, with time to spare after Granada, didn't drive through the ruddy olive-pricked mountains to Cordoba. At the heart of the enchanting, maze-like old quarter, across an extensive courtyard of fountains and orange trees, one enters the city's ancient mosque, the Mezcita. Row after row of mesmerising, double horse-shoe arches, supported on smooth marble columns, radiate in every direction, producing a sense of quiet wonder and hypnotic calm.

# Maureen Barry

## Last Stronghold of the Moorish Kings

When I was told that just an hour's drive from the razzle-dazzle of the Costa del Sol was an oasis of unexploited "wild country" I found it very hard to believe. I was given the tip off about the Alpujarra Alta (that's the wild bit, the Alpujarra Baja is rather like a Moorish Garden of Eden) by a Spanish friend, who considered that the Spanish equivalent of "see Naples and die" was "see Granada and the Alpujarras" - and leave the rest of Andalucia to the coach parties.

The bucolic Andalusian valley known as the Alpujarras - the last stronghold of the Moorish kings in Spain - lies just a mountain range away from the glittering coastal strip and yet has remained surprisingly untamed, virtually unexplored and un-tourist trammelled. Often described as one of the most inaccessible areas of Spain, sandwiched between the Sierra Nevada and the Contraviesa chain along the sea coast, the region is hardly spoiled, and with a road that resists upgrading and a wealth of exotic flora and fauna on either side, it is the perfect place to find a peculiarly Spanish brand of peace and quiet.

When Spain's last Moorish ruler, the Boy King Boabdil - el Rey Chico - was booted out of Granada by Ferdinand and Isabella in 1492, together with his manipulative mother Ayesha, he was granted the fiefdom of this verdant valley to the south of Granada. As young Boabdil left the scintillating city he turned for one last lingering look at a spot known today as the Suspiro del Moro, the Moor's Sigh. In the way of manipulative mothers everywhere, Ayesha reproved him: "You weep like a woman for what you could not hold as a man." It must have been difficult for Boabdil to turn his back on the glories of Granada. Inscribed on the ramparts of the legendary Alhambra are the words:

> *Give him alms, lady, alms,*
> *For there is no pain in life so cruel*
> *As to be blind in Granada.*

Nature was generous with Granada's setting, placing it at the foot of three low mountain spurs, from where the city stretches gracefully up to a luminous horizon with the grandiose backdrop of the Sierra Nevada to the south-east; from the north the elegant Darro, a mountain stream, winds through the city between the Alhambra and Albaicin hill. Granada - its name comes from the Moorish "Karnattah" and not from the Spanish for pomegranate, "granada", which has been adopted as the city's arms - basked in a golden age as capital of Moorish Al-Andalus for over two and a half centuries. As neighbouring Muslim kingdoms failed, Granada prospered. The fertile, irrigated vega to the west provided the Caliphs with a lavish table. As the arts, science and humanities flourished, Granada reached its material, intellectual and spiritual apogee in the triumphant creation of the Alhambra. "Al Qal'a al-Hambra" the "Red Fort" sits on a ridge on top of a wooded hill, the most imaginative and exquisitely delicate man-made fortress ever to be built on a natural fortification.

This is what people come to Granada to see and no amount of description can do justice to its refinement and subtlety, precisely because the essence of Moorish art is its simplicity.

Millions of visitors come to Granada and miss the finest garden in Spain, the Generalife, the Alhambra's garden of seduction, a mass of hedges, shrubs, orange trees and flowers, a perfect spot for romance and indiscretion. Rumour has it that Boabdil's sultana kept assignations here with her lover Hamet, and screened by tamarisks, overpowered by the scent of orange blossom, who could possibly blame them?

The Albaicin, on a hillside facing the Alhambra, has preserved some of the atmosphere of Al-Andalus. This is the oldest quarter of Granada, the haven to which the Moors fled when the Christians conquered the city, and for centuries it was the poorest. Now its tangle of Andalusian alleys hide simple whitewashed homes, with long walls screening gardens as luxuriant as anything the Caliphs lovingly tended.

From beyond the Albaicin hill comes the heartstopping sound of flamenco. These are the notorious caves of Sacromonte - the home of Granada's gypsy population for several centuries. Gypsies expelled from north-west India by Tamerlane found their way to Spain where their rhythms blended with those of the Arabs and Jews to form flamenco; through the group's shared persecution and exile, suffering and isolation, pride and pain, flamenco grew. "Over here, Ma'am, best dancers..." "I tell your fortune, Lady, you have lucky face..." nowadays Sacromonte's flamenco is more à la turista than à la Andaluz. Dinner on the Albaicin is an experience not to be missed; El Ladrillo fills a whole plaza with tables and serves up vast quantities of fish and wine at bargain prices, while the somewhat trendy Cocetin de Ia Parron on the Plaza Larga tries to outdo them in seafood and gazpacho.

From everywhere in Granada mountains peer over, tempting you to explore the jagged snowy wall of the Sierra that hides the valley of the Alpujarras. I was told to dress warmly, for the Sierra Nevada, as the name implies, are snowbound nearly all the year, and even in July and August when the road is clear, it's still chilly at 11,000 feet above sea level. The highest peak, Mulhacen, is less than 40 kms from the coast. At Veleta you enter the Solynieve ski area and then if you are adventurous and the road is clear you continue down into the valley of the Alpujarras. You don't have to chance the mountainous route from Granada, of course; if you prefer you can use the Alpujarras's front door by way of Motril on the coast to Lanjaron, the only real tourist centre of the region. Lanjaron is a well-known spa, and produces most of the mineral water drunk in Spain.

Arriving in the Alpujarras is like entering a time warp; the purity of the Moorish architecture and the customs native to this area have persisted because of the isolation in which the Alpujeños lived until quite recently. Veiled women drew their water at the village pump at Ugijar until 20 years ago and each white village was completely self-contained; to marry into another village was to marry among foreigners. Only the Algerian and Moroccan Atlas has the same style of architecture as the Alpujarras - the flat-roofed two-storeyed houses join on to each other haphazardly and appear to slide down the slopes of the Sierra like melting candlewax. The roofs are made of heavy stone slabs which keep the walls firm during the odd tornado which can blow up in the colder months.

In the open-fronted azotea or attic room of the village houses, corn cobs, sliced egg-plants, strings of red peppers and tomatoes are hung up to dry. While I was admiring a particularly spectacular display of suspended goodies in one azotea in Yegen, the lady of the house, Tia Ana, invited me inside to see her storeroom. The room was next to the kitchen and was a place of great importance. Two or three hundred pounds of grapes hung from the ceiling keeping fresh until the Spring, but becoming more shrunken and sweeter with each passing month; quinces, oranges, lemons and apples were stored, along with pots of green fig jam, rows of ripening persimmons which would be eaten with a spoon when squashy; jars of home-cured olives and of dried apricots and figs, chick peas, lentils and all sorts of beans in large baskets. There were one or two of the famous Alpujarra hams, rubbed regularly with salt to preserve them through the summer months and of course onions, onions hanging everywhere, for *"olla sin cebolla, es baile sin tamborin"* - a stew without onions is like a dance without a tambourine.

To complete my tour Tia Ana showed me her kitchen, with its charcoal stove set into a tiled shelf, stone sink and mellow walnut cupboards. I commented on the sprig of elder hanging at the window to ward off witches. Tia Ana nodded sagely. The Alpujeños are wildly superstitious and revel in tales of witches and warlocks, hechiceras and hechiceros, who fly about on dark nights giving off the sound of sweet music as they pass. A mortar and pestle is the witches' standby, next to the frying pan and way ahead of the kettle in culinary importance, and used now mainly (and very seriously) for making love potions. Tia Aria showed me the garden where herbs medicinal and herbs amatory went into the making of her famous simples. Trevelez, 5,000 feet above the sea, has a great reputation for witchcraft, they even say that its famous hams sold at Fortnum's and Harrods owe their particular flavour to the spells said over them.

That evening in Yegen I ate a marvellous cazuela - a stew of rice, potatoes, green vegetables, meat, tomatoes, pimentos, onions and garlic, powdered almonds and saffron, named after the pot it is cooked in. Choto al ajillo, baby goat with garlic, is another Alpujarran speciality, the Trevelez ham stewed with beans is rated highly and the sweets are very sweet, of the Moorish kind. A strange concoction is migas, a sort of porridge fried in olive oil, garlic and water. Some diners seemed to favour migas with sardines while others preferred hot chocolate poured over it, and I even saw the two served together.

Among the villages of the highest and loveliest part of the region, after leaving Ugijar, are Soportujar with its primeval oak groves, then Pampaneira, Bubion and Capileira, all within sight of each other along the edge of the beautiful ravine called Barranco de Poqueira. Trevelez on the slopes of Mulhacen claims to be the highest village in Europe as well as being renowned for its snow-cured Serrano ham, raved about by gourmets everywhere. At Berchules you can watch the art of carpet weaving, unchanged since Moorish times. Ten kilometres farther on the village of Yegen became famous as the home of British writer Gerald Brenan, a young man anxious to educate himself on a limited income. He imported two thousand books, became something of a local curiosity and received the likes of Lytton Strachey and Virginia Woolf. Times have changed since 1919, even in the backward Alpujarras, when Brenan paid his housekeeper one peseta a day.

Everywhere in the Alpujarras you are made to feel welcome; even when there is no-one in sight the overhanging trees, the wild flowers, vines and donkeys come right to the road's edge to greet you. Spanish hospitality, especially here with the Arab touch, can be overwhelming; people will invite you to their homes, or press you to share their peasant lunch of rough bread, olives, home cured ham and red wine at ease among the olive groves. "Over the mountain" as the locals say, lies the coast and another world; a fortuitous mountain that has helped preserve this valley as an enduring stronghold of Spain's Moorish heritage.

## Recommended Reading

### Andalucia.
by Michael Jacobs. Pallas Athene. ISBN: 1873429266
Excellent mix of background reading and practical information
from a foremost writer on Spain.

### South from Granada. Gerald Brenan
Penguin Publications. ISBN: 0140167005
Classic Brenan account of his life in a tiny Alpujarran village,
and his trips to neighbouring cities such as Granada.

### Alhambra: a Moorish Paradise. Gabrielle van Zuylen, Claire de Virieu Thames and Hudson. ISBN: 0500019738

### Moorish Spain. Richard Fletcher
Phoenix Press. ISBN: 1842126059

## General Information

### andalucia.com
This local Tourist Board site gives details of local fiestas, city
guides, villages of interest, culture and entertainment throughout
Andalucia. Also an excellent resource for seeking out hotels and
accommodation of all types throughout the region.

### islamicart.com
Provides a complete overview of Islamic art and architecture from
all over the world, whilst highlighting specific examples from the
Moorish buildings in Spain with illustrative photographs. Invaluable
if you are to have a better understanding of what you are looking
at once you arrive.

**GreatBuildings.com/buildings/The_Alhambra.html**
Detailed architectural information and photography from the
Alhambra Palace in Granada.

## Specialist Travel Operators

### British Museum Traveller
The intellectual approach to Moorish Spain. The British Museum
offers a specialist tour to Spain's Islamic highlights, accompanied
by a professional lecturer.
See britishmuseumtraveller.com; Tel: 020 7436 7575

### Page and Moy
A Moorish tour that includes trips to delightful Carmona, the
famous Andalucian white villages, Cadiz and Jerez
See page-moy.co.uk; Tel: 08700 106240

### Granada Travel Centre
A specialised local operator based in Granada, offering a variety
of tours around the major sights.
See granadatravel.net; Tel: +34 958 806067

## Accommodation/UK based

### Individual Travellers Spain
Self-catering cottages and rural houses throughout Andalucia.
See indiv-travellers.com; Tel: 08700 773773

### Simply Travel
Hotels, villas and farmhouses in off the beaten track locations
within reach of the main Moorish sights.
See simply-travel.com; Tel: 020 8541 2200

## Hotels of Interest

**Granada.** The city's Parador occupies a stunning location within the grounds of the Alhambra Palace. See parador.es

**Seville.** A favourite is Las Casas de la Juderia, a charming small hotel set around flower filled courtyards. Needs to be booked well in advance in high season. Callejon de dos Hermanas 7.
Tel: +34 95 4415150

**Cordoba.** The Hotel Marisa is small and uncomplicated. Its perfect location offers rooms with views directly onto the Mezcita walls. Cardenal Herrero 6. Tel: +34 957 473142

## Getting There

**Iberia**: from London Airports to Malaga and Seville
**British Airways**: to Seville
**EasyJet:** to Malaga
**Go**: to Malaga

THINGS TO DO 'BEFORE YOU DIE' No. 533

*Andalucia*
"Whether you're gazing at the lacy lattice work and maze of gardens in Granada's Alhambra, sitting under orange trees eating tapas or watching the locals do their intricate hand ballet dances in late night bars in Seville, or sipping sherry in a bodega in Jerez, Andalucia is a rich blend of history, Moorish architecture and rollicking good fun." *Melissa Rossi*

# Green Spain

# Green Spain

Spain, a dusty country of parched plains, arid mountains and lazy Mediterranean beaches. A flash of green in spring after a sprinkling of rain, and that's it, every scrap of vegetation has been scorched into oblivion again by the end of May. So it would appear if one's only experience of the Spanish countryside was from the window of a plane above Madrid, or a quick trip into the hills behind Malaga or Alicante. Yet rolling across the top of the Iberian peninsular, all year round, there is a thick belt of deep green countryside, so deliciously fecund in places that it puts even the English countryside to shame.

Beginning with the Basque Country in the far north-west, crossing Cantabria, Asturias, and ending above Portugal in Galicia, these four autonomous regions epitomise the concept of 'different Spains', with many different peoples. The Galicians are Celts, living off some of the world's best sea-food, in a land often compared to Ireland, only with eucalyptus, vineyards and Scandinavian fjords. Asturias is all rugged mountains and exotic, hidden coves, like Cornwall or Wales some say, but again the comparison is misleading. Cantabria has sweeping beaches and swooping, velvety hills.

The Basque country, and principally the sub-regions of Guipuzcoa and Vizcaya, is the deepest green of them all. With their own government, their own taxes and their ancient language taught in schools, the Basques have ensured that their rich artistic and culinary culture has a permanent foothold. Bilbao's Guggenheim is undoubtedly the gem of modern European architecture; in San Sebastian you'll eat the the most decorous and appetising tapas ('pintxos') in Spain. The small, coastal resorts are definitely worth exploring, in particular Zarautz and Hondarribia, where you should push the boat out, and stay in the magnificent castle Parador.

It is a long standing ambition of mine to find the time to cross these green lands in one fell swoop. Not racing around a region at a time by car, but slowly, and I can think of no better way of doing so than by train or on foot. Regional trains run right across the north coast of Spain, weaving lazily through hills and pastures, and emerging every now and again for a run along the wild Atlantic shore. But best of all would be to follow the northern, 'primitive' route of the Santiago Way, the ancient pilgrim's trail. Many times in the north I've stumbled across the traditional way-marking, a yellow shell on a blue sign, pointing into woodland, or down a quiet coastal path, and thought 'one day, one day.....'

# Maureen Barry

―――――

The melancholy skirl of the bagpipes echoing down a misty glen made my spine tingle with a strong sense of deja-vu. For Celtic Galicia, isolated on the rim of Europe in the far north-western corner of Spain, has more than the climate and an abundance of names prefixed with 'O' in common with the west of Ireland. Verdant Galicia's mountain ranges enclose narrow valleys where the streams jump with trout, chiselled rocky fingers or "rias" indent the coastline, while its people share a Gaelic intensity for their poetic national language and a folklore steeped in superstition and the supernatural.

The Celtic invaders of 1,000 BC must have felt immediately at home in this rain-swept green land facing the setting sun. The Moors left no mark on Galicia and for centuries the province developed out of the mainstream of Spanish life. The result, for the visitor used to seeing Spain through sun-tinted glasses, is a fascinating time-warp, a sense of stepping back into history.

The Galicians, or Gallegos, hemmed in by Portugal and with none of the Spanish lands of the Requistadores to expand into, were forced to turn inwards and divide their land up into smaller and smaller holdings. Today bright green vegetation covers every inch of cultivable land, enclosed by the granite fences each Gallego has erected round his little plot. The area has always been poor and as soon as the New World was opened up Gallegos left in droves for the Americas; there are said to be more Gallegos in

Buenos Aires alone than in Galicia.

Yet the charm of Galicia lies in its idiosyncracy. After a scenic drive from Bilbao through the rugged grandeur of Asturias I suddenly found myself enfolded in the sweep of Galicia's green valleys. On an upland road that wove around the landscape following the line of least resistance I was brought to a halt by a swaying flock of full-uddered cows, leisurely chivvied by an old man with a sprig of wild flowers in his buttonhole. Galicia very evidently proceeds at its own pace and according to its own values. With exquisite courtesy Jose Manuel accompanied me to his hamlet's only bar where I sampled crusty rye bread, cured beef (cecina) and beef chorizo, washed down with a jug of the local Albarino wine.

We passed Jose Manuel's sturdy, self-sufficient farm, with its conical hayrick, its trellis of vines (producing excellent white wines similar to Portugal's "green" wines, like Ribero, Albarino and Condado) and the small plot where he grew turnips, peppers, maize, peas, cabbage and Spain's finest potatoes. Jose Manuel's farm was grand enough to have a monumental granite granary or horreo set up on pillars, topped with a gabled roof and a cross. His sheltered garden boasted oranges, kiwi fruit, palm trees and blooming camellias, which have run riot here since their introduction from Japan. The hills around this little Eden were covered with chestnut, oak and furze forests, while nearer the sea pine and eucalyptus grew in lush profusion to the water's edge.

Gallegos do not have the urban instinct of their fellow Spaniards and most of the population is spread out in some 30,000 villages of 100-200 people. Sprinkled here and there in prime positions are the showy bungalows of the Americanos, returned with bulging wallets from the New

World. Many of the older houses along the coast have elaborate glassed-in balconies or gallerias; La Coruña is famous for them. A distinctive feature of the landscape are the forts or castros the Celts built in the most unlikely and inaccessible places, on mountain tops or with their backsides half into the sea, while the symbols they carved into rock have been adopted by the present day political radicals.

The Galician language has no Celtic roots, being more of a close relation to Portuguese, but it has fought a continuing battle for recognition. En Gallego por favor (in Galician please) implore the wall posters, while signposts in Castilian Spanish have been crossed out and the Galician version substituted. Now Galician is officially recognised, it is compulsory in schools and has its own newspapers and television programmes.

Driving from Jose Manuel's farm through the province of Lugo I was never out of sight of water; lakes and springs feed rivers, brooks and streams which flow so fast that their curiously short names seem appropriate. Three letter words are enough - *Sil, Sor, Iso, Ull, Lor, Mao, Tea* - all of them an angler's paradise covering a thousand-kilometre network of bucolic trout streams.

The Sierra de Ancares in Lugo is an area of outstanding natural beauty. Gorse, heather and cranberry cover the open areas and ancient forests of oak, hazel and holly grow higher up. In the villages of the Sierra you can see primitive "pallozas", round stone houses with thatched roofs where family life still revolves around the fireplace in the centre of the room. Wolf, roe deer and wild boar roam these mountains and in the spring the capercaillie, king of the forest, screams his mating call. Regular folk festivals are traditional in the villages, when the Gallegos, rigged out in national costume, dance the "muneira" and the "pandeira" to the music of the "gaita" or bagpipes, timbrel and castanets. Semi-wild horses live in the mountains between Baiona and A Guarda and their periodic round-up and branding gives another excuse for a round of lively fiestas.

It has been said that the littoral of Galicia has everything: miles and miles of the spectacular, the beautiful, the rugged, the fascinating and the unexpected. The Cantabrian beaches of the north are enormous and popular, while farther south near Fisterra are the less accessible, violent and beautiful beaches for brave bathers. Between Xallas and the Miño the land and sea intertwine in perfect symbiosis; the coast becomes softer and sandier. The vast beach at A Lanzada is a favourite with local Catholic matrons, as a dip in the water is supposed to cure sterility.

But wherever one finds oneself in Galicia all roads lead to Santiago. Santiago de Compostela of the emotive name exploded onto the tourist map as long ago as the eleventh century. The legend began in the year 812 when a monk discovered the lost bones of St James in a field in western Galicia, guided there by the light of a star. Thus Campus Stellae - the Latin for "field of the star" - and the title Santiago de Compostela. St James' bones were all the rage and the pilgrimage to Santiago became one of the great acts of faith of the Middle Ages. At the peak of its popularity in the fourteenth century over half a million pilgrims a year, amongst them Chaucer's *Wife of Bath*, made the perilous journey to the shrine, to claim indulgences from Purgatory and the right to wear the scallop shell emblem of the saint. If the road to Santiago was the first mass travel destination, then the first tour guide, Codex Calixtinus, was written in 1130 by a French monk, Amery de Picaud, offering the pilgrims advice on where not to drink the water, where to find a decent bed for the night and how to avoid muggers.

Today's pilgrims shouldn't encounter such problems, for Galicians are renowned for their hospitality and refined cuisine. Indeed *la cocina gallega* is generally conceded to be the best in Spain. After viewing the baroque splendours of Santiago's cathedral, what better place to unwind than in the Hotel de los Reyes Catolicos next door, a former hostel for pilgrims and now converted into a state-owned Parador of the most shameless luxury. The food, in the arched subterranean restaurant, is exquisite. Galician shellfish is considered to be the best in Europe: lobster, cockles, mussels, shrimp, oysters, crab, octopus, barnacles and ugly creatures you cannot name, plus hake, bream, turbot, lamprey, eel, sardines and scallops feature on every menu and are especially good in the seafood cafes that line Santiago's medieval side streets.

Get up early in the morning so as not to miss the fresh fish auction in the "Muro" market in La Coruña, one of the most important places in the world for direct sales. Seafood farming has become a major industry in Galicia with live turbot and lobster arriving as far afield as Japan in less than 24 hours. Everywhere in Galicia eating is a pleasure. In the family restaurants and marisqueiros in the towns and villages of the hinterland you will find food cooked with love. Specialities are empañadas, a sturdy pie of bread dough with a variety of savoury filling, caldo Gallego, a broth of greens, turnips and white beans, or a hearty winter dish, lacon con grelas (pork shoulder with greens, sausages and potatoes). Cheeses to try are the semi-hard Cebrero and the smoked San Simon, or the soft Tetilla and Ulloa for immediate consumption. Irresistible for dessert is the tarta de almendras (almond tart) topped off in proper fashion with a glass of Galician firewater, orujo, burned with lemon peel and sugar to become the famous "queimada".

Nothing in Galicia is cultivated with such loving care as the grape vine. The Galicians themselves believe their most characterful wine comes from Condado de Salvatierra and El Rosal, bordering the River Miño and the Portuguese frontier. There is general agreement that the most outstanding of all Galician wine is the white Albarino from the Val de Salnes, introduced from the Rhine by Benedictine monks from Cluny during the twelfth century. Probably the best way for the visitor to sample the little-known wines of Galicia is while lingering over a platter of glorious seafood, relax, sip and savour, relying on the expertise of the restaurateur who will have bought direct from a favourite grower. Buen provecho!

# Benjamin Curtis

### Letter from Asturias

If you take a walk along the beach at Gandia, a small Mediterranean resort town an hour to the south of Valencia, at nine o'clock in the morning in July, a surprising sight awaits you. The entire front line, the 'Primera Linea', that long stretch of beach at the water's edge, is already completely occupied by parasols and beach mats, yet there isn't a soul to be seen. The canny Spanish holiday-maker stole down at dawn, marked out his territory, and went back to bed. The effect is rather eerie, and certainly frustrating for the despondent family that arrives half an hour too late: "Look Mama", sighs a small boy, "the sea has all been reserved."

And so it is for all the Spanish Mediterranean coast. The 'Primera Linea' has long since been reserved, marked out, built on and altogether gobbled up. The resort chain from Catalonia to Gibraltar is all but complete, with barely a missing link. In places it is mercifully low-rise and low-key, backed by orange groves and as distinctly Spanish as it was before the builders arrived. But in general the beaches are as packed and no less hectic than the Metro in Madrid, the sun is merciless and the humidity at night will make an insomniac of even the deepest of sleepers.

The sage Spanish traveller knows to head to the north coast instead. After a dip into the hot swarthy baths of the Med, a trip to Asturias brings immeasurable relief, like putting in some ear plugs and turning on the cold tap.

Bordered by the more popular provinces of Galicia and Cantabria, and cut off from the centre of the country by the formidable Picos de Europa mountain range, Asturias has been all but forgotten, not a single 'Apart-Hotel' complex in sight.

Yet this is a land straight from the pages of a fairy tale. The mountains are so fierce and sit so close to the coast that you imagine them put there by some imaginative storyteller, who would have giants sliding down them each morning for a quick wash in the sea. The foothills behind the cliffs are so green, the cows that graze them so picture-perfect and the woodlands and vegetable patches so ornate, that one would hardly be surprised to stumble across Hansel and Gretel, or houses made of chocolate.

The people that inhabit this dreamy landscape are no less magical themselves. In the mountains, lottery sellers walk from village to distant village with strings of tickets around their necks, as eagerly as their city partners dart from bar to bar in busy urban streets. In tiny village fiestas they jump blindfold into a ring and tumble helplessly after squealing greasy piglets. Late one night in a roadside tavern I came across a drunk, elfish old man who filled the room with clouds of smoke from every long drag on his cigarette.

"Still walking back to Ribadesella tonight then?" the waitress teased him. This involved a journey of some thirty miles along the pitch-black coast. He filled the room with smoke again in reply. He could, he was saying, if he wanted, and I wouldn't be surprised if he did.

The Asturians eat extraordinary bowls of rich bean and sausage stews, and drink cider for breakfast, lunch and supper, poured from earthy bottles held high above the head in one hand, into a glass held well below the waist in the other, eyes looking neither up nor down, but strictly dead ahead. Over the years they have shown ruthless powers of resistance. It is said that in the eighth century some thirty Asturians kept an army of 400,000 Moors out of their mountains, and as such this remained the only part of Spain not to fall under Moorish rule.

Now, it seems, they feel under threat from a new invasion, just as numerous and no less alarming. "Presidents!" snarled one waiter ominously, after he'd explained the dishes of the day. "They are coming from Madrid, presidents of enormous corporations, buying big houses. They have more money than you could imagine. More come every year, building their palaces on our land". Could the unthinkable happen? Could Asturias fall prey to the worst excesses of the Mediterranean?

It's doubtful. Even if the locals don't send them packing then the weather will. A beach holiday in Asturias is a gamble that most Spaniards are not prepared to accept: for every day of sun, you may well have two of rain. But risk it, and you will lie on the most beautiful beaches in Spain.

Backed by eucalyptus groves and cliffs carpeted in tropical greens, they are populated by foraging goats, peaceful locals, perhaps a stray Victorianesque English family playing cricket with driftwood, and silent nudists who take refuge behind a rocky outcrop down at the far end. The Cantabrian Sea is absolutely pure and invigoratingly cool, its waves endlessly ruffling the fine sand at the shore.

Back in Gandia, at six in the evening, many of the 'Primera Linea' sunbathing elite have retreated to their high-rise bunkers, as tanned as leather. A few elderly bathers flounder amongst the strips of plastic bag that somehow find their way into the tepid lifeless sea. It's aerobics time and a large section of sand has been cordoned off for 200 teenagers who jump, sway and sweat this way and that, to the disco sounds of a monstrous sound-system that can be heard half a mile away. This is hellish and yet no-one seems to mind, the power of the sun, it seems, having blinded their judgment. Long then, I quietly hope, may it continue to rain in Asturias.

## Recommended Reading

**The Pilgrimage Road to Santiago : The Complete Cultural Handbook. David Gitlitz, Linda Kay Davidson**
St. Martin's Press. ISBN: 0312254164

**The Basque History of the World. Mark Kurlansky**
Jonathan Cape. ISBN: 0099284138
An extremely thorough and engaging text on Basque history, politics, and culture.

**Spain: The Rough Guide**
Rough Guides. ISBN: 1858288703

## General Information

**tourspain.es/turespae/banvef.htm**
A general run down (in Spanish) on all four regions from the Spanish Tourist Board. The site gives a good geographical overview and lists each region's highlights.

The following web sites each provide excellent regional information, including cultural activities, fiestas, leisure, sports, trips of interest and maps. They also provide excellent accommodation sections, an invaluable resource for the independent traveller:

**Galicia**: galinor.es
**Asturias**: asturnor.com
**Cantabria**: turismo.cantabria.org
**Basque County**: spaintour.com/basque.htm

## Specialist Travel Operators

### Inntravel
Walking holidays in Northern Spain, including the well known 'From the Picos to the sea' walk in Asturias, that treks from the Picos de Europa mountains down to the coast, staying in 'casonas', traditional stone farm houses, along the way. inntravel.co.uk; Tel: 01653 629000

### Travellers Way
A wide range of holidays in rural houses and hotels throughout the region. travellersway.co.uk; Tel: 01527 578000

### Auto Plan
Motoring holidays to a selection of holiday accommodation, specialising particularly in Galicia and the Picos de Europa. autoplanhols.co.uk; Tel: 01543 257777

## Accommodation/local

### guiarural.com
This recently launched Spanish web site contains a data base with details of a growing number of rural houses in all four regions.

## Accommodation/UK based

### Spanish Affair
A company offering a range of farmhouses, cottages and villas in Asturias and Cantabria.spanishaffair.com; Tel: 020 73858127

### Casas Cantabricas
A long-standing, family run company offering carefully chosen houses throughout Cantabria, Asturias and Galicia. Tel: 01223 328721.

## Hotels of Interest

**The Paradors at Hondarribia** (Basque Country), and **Santiago de Compostela** (Galicia) offer affordable luxury in incredible venues, a medieval castle and renaissance convent respectively. See the Parador web site for details: parador.es

## Getting There

**Brittany Ferries**: Plymouth to Santander in 24 hours (Brittany Ferries also offer holidays and accommodation in the region.) See brittany-ferries.co.uk; Tcl: 08705 360360
**P & O Ferries**: Portsmouth to Bilbao in 36 hours
See poportsmouth.com; Tel: 08705 980555
**Iberia**: from London airports to Santiago de Compostela, Oviedo and Bilbao
**British Airways**: to Bilbao
**Go**: to Bilbao

# Untamed Spain

# Untamed Spain

When you cross the Pyrenees from France into Spain, something changes, almost imperceptibly at first. If you come, as I first did, from Andorra, you may notice that the mountains are a little more rugged, the streams more bubbling and the towns somehow less cozy and manicured. Below the high peaks you'll find tiny, precarious B-roads winding through sun-baked, Martian hills, which peter out eventually into rolling plains. This, you'll soon conclude, isn't like any part of Europe you've ever known before.

Wild country is everywhere in Spain, in beautiful Extremadura, where Jasper Winn rides with the Spanish Cowboys, where ancient towns built on Roman foundations with pillaged South American silver, slowly crumble away. In Guadix, near Granada, you'll find half the population happily living in the hillside, in carefully burrowed cave homes, complete with running water, a constant year-round temperature, and satellite TV. Spain boasts lynxes, ibex, wild boar, pink flamingos and bears. Half the wild flower species in Europe can be found in Spain.

The culture, though some of the more unpleasant elements have filtered through, is equally un-northern European. Tumultuous, heart-wrenching Flamenco guitar permeates the radio waves and echoes in Granada's cave-bars, whilst Sevillanas, the intoxicating, lusty flamenco-esque dance, sets southern fiestas alight in summer. Come to any of the major cities, and you'll find courses to teach you both. Then there are the great Pilgrimages with an unsettlingly hedonistic air, the pig slaughters, 'matanzas', in winter, and of course, the ubiquitous bullfight, just as popular as ever, as Kamin Mohammadi recounts below.

Untamed Spain lies in the interior, in provinces such as Aragon, Almeria, Extremadura and Castilla and Leon. It hides in the quieter towns too, like Teruel, Zamora, and Cartagena, and in the lesser known Sierras, such as Gredos, and the Pena de Francia below Salamanca. Visit any of these, and you will discover pure contemporary wilderness. And if, like Mark Hudson below, you get seduced into buying a place - so romantic, so cheap, such good value! - beware...

# Kamin Mohammadi

## Blood and Sand

The sun poured onto the saffron sand, picking out crimson. A hush had descended on the 19th century auditorium as the man in the sparkling suit, head held low, eyes intent, drew out a sword from behind his cape, gaze fixed on the huge creature in front of him; a panting, angry bull, pawing the ground and snorting while the blood splashed down from the web of muscles encircling its massive neck. Six hundred kilos of testosterone concentrated into two frighteningly large, wide horns, with points as sharp as sabres, facing a lithe slip of a man squeezed into a tight suit, his only defence a red cape, and the sword. He held the bull motionless in front of him by the sheer force of his stare.

Slowly the matador raised his weapon, turning his body so that his whole energy was directed through it in an arc. As the audience hushed he surged forward and in one movement sank the sword into the bull's neck, to its hilt. The animal danced in a confused circle while the man stood motionless, holding its gaze. As the bull's knees started to buckle, the creature suddenly burst forward with its last gasp of life, but the matador did not flinch. He raised a hand and, the tenacious look still pinning the bull, slowly lowered his outstretched arm, inches away from the top of the bull's head. With this movement, almost at the matador's command, the bull sank at his feet. For a split second before it died, before the thunderous applause and waving of white handkerchiefs erupted, the bull and the man were held in a

162

perfect moment, the fight over, strange comrades in the curious ballet that is bullfighting.

Bullfighting is big business in Spain today. It is estimated that 150,000 people are in some way involved in the industry. Despite the condemnation of international animal welfare groups, shifts in attitude have been slow in coming. The owners of the 300 bull breeding farms represent a powerful lobby group, receiving subsidies from the EU and exemption from the 1998 amendment to the Treaty of Rome which covers animal welfare. In 1996 the Ministry of Culture provided nearly 40 million pesetas to support the corrida. This does not include the subsidies given to individual bullrings by local and regional councils. In 1998 the total number of fights staged in Spain, France and Portugal reached 1,813, almost 200 up on the previous year. After the slump in popularity witnessed in the 1980s, bullfights are on the rise again.

The reasons are legion. The young people of Spain are becoming impressed with bullfighting again, the language of the fight part of their hip patter. Television pays big money for major bullfighting events; indeed it is hard to escape the corrida during the season, which runs from April to October. Matadors are revered as rock stars, mobbed at every turn, followed around by groupies and comfortable showing off their homes in the glossy pages of *¡Hola!* Populist young matadors like Jesulin de Ubrique and El Cordobes attract hordes of young people, women especially. This generation of new matadors has a particularly common touch, and they are as disliked by purists as they are by the anti-fight lobbies.

Jesulin de Ubrique even staged a fight just for women: almost 10,000 women packed the ring and the television coverage received record ratings. Purists fear that such displays are turning the fight into a circus, that the original art form - the supposedly great, glorious and mystical fight between man and beast - will be cheapened.

The origins of the bullfight lie in a region of wild mountainous beauty in the Andalusian interior, in the White Town of Ronda. This was the birthplace of the Maestranza, an order of knights that laid down the rules of early bull-fighting on horseback, an aristocratic pastime. Legend has it that in the 18th century, Francisco Romero jumped into the ring when an aristocrat had been unseated by a bull, distracting the animal by waving his cap. The crowd loved this display of clowning bravery and the modern bullfight was born. The Romero family embellished it further; Francisco's son Juan is credited with organising the matador's team. However, it was Francisco's grandson, Pedro Romero, who, in 1785, laid down and demonstrated the rules of the fight in the newly built Plaza de Toros with his series of passes and moves, many of which are still in use today. Fighting well into his seventies, Romero killed about 6,000 bulls in his ring, and died at the age of 90, having never been gored.

Each corrida begins with a procession. To the accompaniment of the paso doble, two mounted, traditionally dressed alguacilillos (constables) lead in the three matadors, followed by the cuadrillas (team) and the bell-bedecked mules that will drag off the dead bulls. With the matadors wearing their traje de luces (suit of lights), followed by three similarly attired banderillos and two picadores mounted on horses wrapped in armour, there is no doubt that this is a splendid spectacle. The fight itself will last some two hours, during which time the three matadors will dispatch two bulls each.

A hush descends as the band announces the imminent entry of the first bull. The door to the enclosure snaps open with a bang and the bull trots ponderously into the ring. The fresh bull is put through its paces by the banderillos and the matadors, who will make some passes to study its movement and pace. Some matadors choose this moment to make their most outrageous and dangerous moves, before the bull is tired or injured.

With another blast of the band's horns, the picadors are led in. These mounted, padded fighters, with their wide-brimmed hats, lances and armoured horses, vividly recall the tradition linking this event with its aristocratic past. The bull is encouraged to charge one of the picadors, who can now attack it with the lance, piercing its neck and back muscles in order to make it lower its head, without which it would be impossibly dangerous to fight on foot. Undeniably the most gruesome part of the corrida, this *suerte de picaris* is intensely disliked by aficionados. For the horse it is clearly not a pleasant experience - its ears are stuffed with rags to shut out the noise of the bull and spectators, its vocal chords may be cut to stop it screaming in pain and it may be injured despite its padding. Also, many picadors are over-zealous in stabbing the bull, leaving it too drained to put up an effective fight. After three such attacks, the horses, blind-folded on the right eye (the one that faces the bull), are led out, and the *suerte de banderillas* is trumpeted in.

The three banderillos take it in turns to place a set of banderillas (darts mounted on coloured shafts) into the bull's neck. The banderillo attracts the bull's attention by moving his own body rather than a cape, so that the bull charges and the two are running towards each other before the banderillo springs up between the bull's horns and stabs the two darts into the bull's neck or back. He then safely moves out of the bull's line of vision, but sometimes a canny animal will chase his tormentor, resulting in an undignified but rather comical leap to safety, recalling Goya's sketches of the ring.

The suerte de matar can now begin. The matador enters the ring alone, having swapped his pink and gold cape for the red muleta. He raises his knotted hat to the president of the fight and the guest of honour, as often as not royalty during the major festivals. He dedicates the bull to either an individual, to whom he tosses his hat, or to the audience - by far the most popular decision, earning instant goodwill from an irreverent crowd - when he places his hat in the centre of the ring. Thus begins the fluid engagement of animal and man that crescendos into a graceful, twirling dance as the matador draws the bull ever closer to his body, sometimes using the bull's haunches as it brushes past to pirouette round and face it again. In reality, of course, such moments are almost as scarce as the clean kill through the heart; the animals often too weak, confused or close to death to engage effectively, or the matador may not make the mental connection with the bull which is necessary to raise the fight into the realm of artistic ritual.

The kill itself is rarely achieved with one thrust of the sword. Usually a dagger is subsequently used to sever the bull's spinal chord, causing instant death. If a bull has been especially brave, the spectators will applaud it heartily at its death. The bull's body is then dragged out by the team of mules. Should a matador have impressed the audience, they will wave white handkerchiefs and demand an award of one ear, two ears and the tail, and the matador will walk around the ring, displaying the trophy to the audience, whose cheers are only matched by their eagerness to shower him with gifts: a variety of objects that range from the customary flower to wineskins, hats and handbags. The highest accolade a matador can receive is to be carried out, shoulder-high, from the ring's main gate by an excited crowd.

Mention cruelty to an aficionado and he will talk of the shoddy practices that in the last few decades have haunted the corrida. Allegations of foul play include shaving of a bull's horns - not only incredibly painful but also disturbing to its sense of balance - to lessen the risk for the matador; the drugging of bulls with sulphates to induce severe pain and further malco-ordination in the ring, or the injection of sedatives. The World Society for the Protection of Animals insists that one of the signs of a civilised society is that there is no gratuitous cruelty to animals for the sake of sport, and talks of educating people.

An aficionado will argue that if the corrida didn't exist, the Lidia breed of bull would die out with it; that the industry has done much in the 1990s to clean up its act and that the corrida is not a sport anyway, it is a cultural event. And sure enough, newspaper reviews of bullfights are found not in the sports section but under culture.

The fight is billed as a contest of life or death, but for the bull there is only certain death. For the matador and the aficionado, however, there is what the Spanish call 'the bull-fighting worm', a worm that enters the brain through the retina and eats you up so all you can think about is the fight. Those with the worm are not hard to find. The King of Spain is one of Spain's great aficionados. The future of bullfighting looks secure.

# Jasper Winn

---

## SPANISH COWBOYS

How far do you have to go to be a cowboy? Well, you've got to wear some pretty damn-fool hats, and learn how to walk in spurs, for a start. But geographically you only have to make it as far as Spain to be able to do some authentic cowboying, and with much better wine than any American ranch has to offer. All this makes sense - the Spanish conquistadors with their horsemanship, gun-backed swagger and habit of filling the freshly subjugated New World with cattle were the root stock for the myth and the reality of the Wild West. And they left plenty of proto-cowboys behind to mind the farm back in Europe.

Even so, I was surprised to find Spanish vaqueros - cowboys - in the western province of Extremadura, were still herding cattle on horseback, moving long-distance between winter grazing grounds in the lowlands and summer pastures high in the Sierra Gredos. Each June around 30,000 head of cattle strike off for the north and fresh grass. Some of the herds number only a few dozen animals, others several hundred. Many of these rebanos cover 300 kilometres or more on their annual trek. For thousands of years this annual transhumance has been the response to a climate described by the Spanish as 'three months of winter and nine months of hell.' It was this combination of weather and movement that created the first cowboys.

Seven years ago I set off, on the first of many trips, to play the B-movie greenhorn. By vowing to ride anything with four legs, I was able to join a bunch of vaqueros on their gruelling cross-country trek through the heart of modern Europe. I had a pair of riding boots, a harmonica and a stockman's hat.

On our first night out, in the darkness before dawn, I pulled my wet blanket closer. Cold rain dripped from my hat brim into the smoke of a sullen fire. I was with a team of cowboys hired to drive 290 of the Marques de Valdueza's pedigree cattle north, and the vaqueros were still mistrustful of this stranger in their midst.

Beyond the feeble light of the flames the cattle shifted restlessly in a discord of brass bells. Dionisio, the head vaquero, stirred himself to walk around the herd; bow-legged, cigarette glowing, whistling softly. Manolo, the horseman, haggard after twelve hours in the saddle and a sleepless night, reached out to shake me fully awake. "Oyga, hombre! Desayuno - breakfast," he croaked, passing me a bottle of brandy.

We drank breakfast before splashing through the mud to tack-up the horses. Emiliano and Fermin were ghostly figures in the rain, urging the couched cattle to their feet. There was the clunking of heavy iron stirrups as we swung up into our saddles, and then the harsh cries of: "Vaca! Vaca! HOOOOOOO-UUUUPP vacas!" As the herd gained momentum the bells on the lead cows rang out louder and the erratic clanging became a regular tolling. The sun was already drying off the ground and our clothes.

Over the following days, as we rode through the heat, I fell into the rhythm of the cattle's slow progress towards the mountains. Our route across the plains, rivers and hills of Extramadura was ordained by long usage, and marked by familiar landmarks. The scimitar-horned, black cattle moved at the speed of a thunder-head across the plains, grazing as they went. And we, riding the flanks, were part of the natural world. Seemingly invisible on our horses we rode amongst azure-winged magpies, great bustard, hoopoes and a hundred other species of birds.

The canadas - cross-country drove roads - which we followed were a unique environment, and the passing of the cattle was an important part of their ecology. Kites and kestrels pounced on insects and rodents flushed out by the pounding of a thousand hooves, and vultures circled down on those cattle, (always from other herds, Dionicio, was quick to point out), that had been lost en route.

Having failed to fully master the rough local cigarettes or the throatfuls of acidic wine spurted from the communal wine skin, my last chance to win acceptance into the inner world of the vaqueros came in the shape of a horse.

Mustapha offered his infrequent riders a menu of upsetting tricks; bucking, rearing or bolting as the fancy took him. I, marked down as cannon-fodder, spent a morning being flung skywards and occasionally picking myself off the ground in a rough-riding style dubbed the "metodo irlandaise" by the fascinated vaqueros. This, due to luck in landing on my feet, they saw as a cunning way of wearing down a difficult horse by dismounting at great speed before resolutely climbing aboard again. It was enough to earn me my spurs in the cowboys' minds, and to give me work on subsequent drives, coaxing awkward horses into something approaching submission. I'd become a card-carrying vaquero.

The life that I came to share with the vaqueros had changed little over the centuries. Long hours in the saddle; stews of chorizo and beans ladled out of a cauldron from atop a campfire; the pleadingly aggressive cries of cante jondo sung as the sun slipped down over Portugal; occasional nights of drinking in village bars; the bleached bones and crumpled hides of dead cows by the side of the track; our herd rucking and brawling on a river bank before plunging wither-deep into the waters.

Though the motivation for the cattle drive was mainly economic - it was cheaper to drive the cattle on foot than to truck them, and made for a finer, leaner meat as well - there was a romantic undercurrent to the trip. The Spanish felt that the transhumance, with its cattle, horses and men moving through a harsh landscape, summed up the soul of their country. Friends of the herds' owner, many of them English, would come out to ride with us at weekends as paying guests. Some of the 'guest vaqueros' rode for longer periods, camping out alongside the herd or staying in local paradors. Most were excellent riders and well-versed in the Spanish skill of having a good time. Impromptu parties would spring up under the trees, with flamenco as the soundtrack, even more and better wine flowing from the botas, and horses being raced alongside the cattle.

The pleasures of the transhumance are those of rural Spain, as they have been for generations. But the dangers are of our own century. No longer the wolves and bandits of the past but now the four lanes of traffic where, for two miserable days, the herd was forced to cross and re-cross the Madrid-Lisbon highway. The vaqueros became Don Quixotes, wracked by chivalry, tilting at the juggernauts and speeding cars with their varras held like lances, forcing the traffic to a halt as we galloped the cattle, packed tight as a can of spam, from one side to another.

It was when we finally breasted the pass of the Puerto

del Pico and the cattle flooded into belly-high grass, that we felt the full magic of the transhumance. Over our 12 day trek we had beaten time itself. We had turned the calendar back from the searing summer of the lowlands to a lush spring that here, high in the mountains, would last until the first snows of winter.

I had entwined my seasons with those of the vaqueros. Having shared the wine, the songs, the jokes, the hardships and the dangers of their trek on my first season cowboying, they counted me as a companero, and assumed I would return. They were right; each spring I sense the tolling of the cow bells, feel my legs bowing to take the shape of a horse and find myself drawn again to Spain, always arriving in time to mount up and ride out behind the cattle.

And since hitting the ground one night in a bar in Navalmoral I've had my character sealed in the clear acrylic of humour-edged legend that passes for history amongst the vaqueros. As Dionicio delights in recounting, I am a remarkable man:

"Un hombre who can ride the worst horses, the most difficult animals, but...and this is strange...," always the long pause and a trago of wine before continuing, "...he gets thrown by a bar stool. Muy raro - very strange?"

# Mark Hudson

———

## A House in Spain

I'm sitting on the terrace of a house in the northern shadow of the Sierra Nevada, looking down over ancient rooftops, as the scrubby hills darken, the bare outlines of the mountains beyond retaining - as they always do at this time of day - an unearthly, lunar radience.

There's something to be said for exploring a country from end to end, ticking off its great sites and getting to grips with its various regions and cultures. And there's something to be said for staying put in one place - whether it's your own property or a villa you're fond of returning to - and letting the essence of the land and the culture seep into you. I've been coming to Spain for ten years, my wife for twenty, and we've barely budged more than a few miles beyond this terrace. Yet Spain has revealed herself to us through flamenco-singing policemen, rowdy village bullfights, through recalcitrant plumbers with endlessly extending mañana schedules, through the charming Hispanic chauvinism of our friends the villagers, and most of all through the fabric and spirit of this house.

It is built, like the rest of the village, from schist, a rust coloured relative of slate shot through with glittering minerals, and roofed in launa, an impermeable mica mud that is dug out of the Sierras and trodden into the roofs on the nights of the waning moon. It's a style of architecture that exists only in this remote corner of Andalucia and in the High Atlas of Morocco - an extraordinary survival of Islamic

173

Africa in Europe.

This place is our bolt-hole on the very edge of Europe, our slice of another world. And we've come here with the sole intention of getting shot of it.

Twenty years ago, my wife and her then boyfriend decided to walk the length of the Sierra Nevada - Spain's biggest mountains - from Almeria to Granada, staying in primitive shelters high in the uninhabited peaks. One Sunday morning, filthy and exhausted, they descended into a village to find a religious procession in progress. Sitting on the edge of the village fountain, munching on bread as the plaster saints were carried past, they fell in love with the place. And they soon learnt that local houses could be bought at prices which, even to them - barely out of university - seemed amazingly low. Within a week they'd bought one in a neighbouring village, a former centre of the Moorish silk industry, that lay among almond groves at the end of a winding track. It was a house out of the peasant dramas of Lorca, with slate floors, big sombre rooms and animals still living on the lower floor - a house whose thick walls seemed to have grown organically from the hard slate beneath.

When their relationship had run its course my wife bought her partner out, and took to spending several months a year here - recovering from the rigours of her job in further education, learning Spanish and becoming part of the community - la chica rubia, 'the fair girl', who tore through the almond groves on her motorbike, skirts billowing. And just as she was beginning to feel that she'd done Spain, and there must be other parts of the world that ought to be explored, I arrived on the scene, and the process of enamoration began all over again.

Here was an opportunity to empathise with the

harshness and extremity of the old Andalucian world - qualities that breathed from the walls of the house and from the worn faces of our neighbours. And amid the glitter of all-night fiestas and the queasy pandemonium of village bullfights, there was the other side of the Spanish coin - the compulsive gaiety. And, of course, there was flamenco. The harsh cry of gypsy song is never as powerful and affecting as when heard in the blazing Andalucian sunlight, the air tinged with the tang of tobacco and baking earth and the aroma of olive oil heating in big black frying pans.

To engage deeply with another culture, to become part of a community that may have values utterly different to our own, is a dream that many of us share. We can't all go the whole hog like our not-too distant neighbour Chris Stewart, whose book *Driving over Lemons*, an account of his trials and triumphs as an Andalucian smallholder, has been a runaway best-seller. Nor can we all throw up our jobs and open a guest house in India like that couple in the TV advert. But as the world becomes smaller and cultural differences are ironed out, so, paradoxically, and perhaps only for a while, this kind of adventure is open to an ever greater number of people.

For many, a second home abroad still just means convenient holidays with plenty of sun and cheap booze. But there are an increasing number who choose properties in the most arid and inhospitable places - and the older and more ruinous the better. Make no mistake, having a second home is, by definition, an indulgence open only to the privileged. Yet for many it is imbued with idealism. Living in another culture means having to open yourself to other ways of thinking and feeling. It is a way of learning, about other peoples, other cultures and, above all, about yourself. And like those other modern rites of passage, backpacking and good works in the developing world, it is best undertaken when you are young and commitment-free or when you've sent your offspring into the world and are ready for a fresh challenge. Because quite apart from the physical and financial demands, living inanother culture requires an enormous amount of emotional energy, commitment and belief.

When you've got young children and a demanding job, and you're mortgaged up to the hilt on a property that may have its own severe structural problems, the last thing you want to do with your all too brief holiday is travel a thousand miles to do battle with absentee plumbers, grumpy electricians and cantankerous civil servants. Your rough-hewn peasant dwelling with its uneven stairs and unfenced terraces reveals itself as terrifyingly child-hazardous. You finally face the fact that decent though your farming neighbours are, you have absolutely nothing in common with them. And the more you withdraw, the more you feel them starting to resent you, till the idea of passing through the village under the disapproving eyes of the black-clad matrons is just one more reason why you don't want to go there.

While we've been growing up, the village itself has changed. Andalucia is no longer the Third World. EC development grants mean that most of the village is now roofed in terra-cotta tiles or corrugated iron. Slate floors and dug-out latrines have given way to marble facing and all mod cons. Ours is now the most primitive house in the village, the only one with its original launa roof. But such a form of architecture requires continual maintenance. A generation ago, every man in the village was effectively a builder. When it rained and the roof leaked, he'd climb up there with a bucket of launa he'd carted down from the Sierras on donkey-back. But when you live a thousand miles away, you can't do that, and the villagers, some of whom now drive better cars than we do, have no interest in doing it for us. Launa is part of a way of life that is fast passing into memory.

We haven't visited the house in nearly five years. The roof is in dire need of repair, and we've heard that the continual leaking is causing one of the rear walls to detach itself from the rest of the house. The electricians who modernised the wiring have ripped great holes out of the walls, and the last friend who went to stay there decamped to a hotel after two days. My wife has developed a dread of thinking about the place. And although she'd love to sell it, arranging viewings for English people who might appreciate the house's romantic appeal and architectural interest will inevitably be complicated and protracted, while to a Spaniard it's just a rustic ruin and practically worthless. When we received a late night phone-call telling us our leaking roof is rotting the beams of our neighbour's animal enclosure and he's planning legal action, we realised something had to be done.

Our Andalucian dream has become a nightmare - a liability we can't afford, a source of anxiety we don't need. Drastic measures are needed. And the ironic thing is, we're probably going to end up selling it back to the woman my wife bought it from, for little more than she aquired it for in the first place.

As we turn the huge iron key - more suited to a dungeon than a domestic abode - and swing open the great studded gate, pushing aside a reef of straw, animal droppings and other rubbish, and peer into the dimness, we have mixed feelings. Our friend who keeps an eye on the place for us, has stacked large areas with her old furniture, the limewashed walls are flaking, a whole interior wall needs replacing and there is death watch beetle in the cedar roof beams. But apart from that, the place isn't in too bad a state.

As I sweep away the years of dust and flaking plaster, mopping the slate slabs to their original blue-black lustre, I reacquaint myself with the sombre, changeless feel of the place. There are occasional erruptions of noise: Mexican soap operas blaring from neighbours' windows, cement-mixers, banging doors and the cawing conversations of women in the street below. But the moment these stop, a profound, almost monumental silence returns, disturbed only by the wind sighing over the roofs and terraces. I inject the roof beams against beetle, and the thought that I may be performing these tasks for the last time is peculiarly saddening.

I keep telling my wife that time is short and she must get the negotiations for the sale underway as soon as possible. But she does nothing about it, and without asking I know why. The mere smell of the place - the sharp, slightly acid tang of sheep and goats, mingling with stone, old mortar and ages of limewash - evokes so many memories and sensations. Particularly there's the exhilaration of discovery, of the place, the people and of each other - of that feeling you have when you're starting out together, creating a world around yourselves. I'd forgotten how important a part of that Spain had been.

Owning this place may be illogical, inconvenient and a drain on our resources. But if you hang onto such a place for a couple of decades, you find that far more of you is bound up with it than you'd have thought, and dispensing with it is not easy. It's not just nostalgia. Both of us have discovered, somewhat to our surprise, that we really do like the place.

As we approached the village on our first evening, driving across the arid plain of Guadix, we experienced again the heart-stopping site of the castle of la Calahorra, its pink sandstone towers bathed in the dusty evening haze, rising against the vast purple backdrop of the Sierras.

We've rediscovered the pleasures of the evening paseo along the castenyar - the chestnut walk - that runs along the bottom of the village, through orchards and gardens watered by ancient Moorish irrigation systems, to the shrine of the village's own Virgin. Every group of villagers has to be greeted and the tone of the response grunted back through the dusky dimness indicates our standing with that section of the community.

Standing in the village square, we gossip with old men who remember my wife's first days in the village, with young women who she dandled on her knee as tots and now have two or three children of their own, some older than our daughter. And we find the villagers remarkably forgiving. Forgiving? Of what? Only of the fact that we haven't spent enough time with them.

On Saturday we go to our local metropolis, the market town of Guadix, that lies in a strange sandstone tableland of mesas and windworn pinnacles. With its Moorish citadel and a cathedral that looks as though it's growing out of the orange rock, Guadix has become a popular stop for tourist coaches. But we like it for its relaxed, workaday atmosphere and because we know it extremely well. We like to have breakfast at the café by the park, with the strollers and market-goers milling around us, before shopping ourselves for things like brooms, shovels and beetle-poison.

I used to sneer at people who went to the same place every year, who liked to have familiar things around them when they went away, who fancied their lifestyle choices had given them a connection with the poor of remote climes. You're English, I would have said to myself as I am today, what has Andalucia to do with you, and you with it? But if you keep going somewhere long enough, you find that it's become something to do with you. It's rather a pleasant realisation. It infers that things naturally and gradually form themselves into a pattern, that everything eventually has some point...

Oh, yes. The house. Have we sold it?

Of course not.

# Untamed Planning

## Recommended Reading

### The New Spaniards. John Hooper
Penguin Publications. ISBN: 0140131914
An excellent round up of Spain and contemporary Spanish culture,
full of mind boggling facts and recent historical events.

### Spain. Jan Morris.
Faber. ISBN: 0140095152
A fascinating, fact-filled account of Spain, its people, cities and
countryside.

### The Face of Spain. Gerald Brenan
Penguin Publications. ISBN: 0140095632
No one has captured the spirit of Spain under Franco so well
as Brenan. Makes you yearn for a time machine.

### Spanish Hours. Simon Courtauld
Libri Mundi. ISBN: 1872037046
Contemplative wanderings around Spain.

### On Bullfighting. A.L. Kennedy
Yellow Jersey Press. ISBN: 0224060996
Excellent on bullfighting history and practice, plus intimate
slices of Granada and Lorca.

### Driving Over Lemons. Chris Stewart
Sort of Books. ISBN: 0953522709
The book that made the Alpujarras famous.

## General Information

### red2000.com/spain/culture-index.html
All about Spain's cultural index includes background information

on the origins and history of Flamenco and the Bullfight, as well as providing a useful selection of internet links.

### mundo-taurino.org
The world of bullfighting explored thoroughly, including a who's who of matadors, and a taurine hall of fame detailing 'illustrious bulls' and bullfighters killed in the ring.

### 6toros6.com
The most prestigious Spanish bullfighting magazine includes updates on recent fights, interviews with the stars, and all the news from the taurine world. In Spanish.

### flamenco-world.com/flamenco.htm
News, reviews and who's who in the world of Flamenco music and dance. You can even download MP3 music files for a taste of Spain's most famous music style.

## Specialist Travel Operators

### Dance Holidays
Learn Flamenco, Sevillanas and Salsa in eleven destinations in Spain including Granada, Seville, Madrid, and beach-side Vejer. See danceholidays.com; Tel: 01293 527722

### Nature Trek
Nature Trek run expert-led botanical and bird watching expeditions to many of the wilder regions of Spain. Example tours include Mountain Flowers of Western Andalucia, Picos and Plains - The Best Of Northern Spain, and Spain's Coto Donana & Extremadura. See naturetrek.co.uk; Tel: 01962 733051

### Holts Tours
Holts historical tours follow in the footsteps of famous battles fought in Spain, such as the Peninsular war in Extremadura,

Roncevalles in the Pyrenees, and the Battle of San Sebastian.
See battletours.co.uk; Tel: 0800 731 1914

## Accommodation

### Secretplaces.com

If you want to really hide away in untamed Spain, try Secret
Places. County estates, monasteries, manor houses and towers
all over Spain, including all the wilder regions, such as Aragon,
Navarra, and Extremadura. Also an excellent source of information
on rural tourism and the geography of specific regions.
See secretplaces.com; Tel: (0035) 1214647430

# Last Word

***

It would have to be September, of course, the most perfect month in Madrid. Early September, when enough of the Madrilenos are still away on holiday, when the city isn't quite up to full speed again, when temperatures have cooled a little from August's dizzying extremes. It's still hot, like an exceptional summer in England, but at least now we can venture outside in the afternoon. Any perfect day in Madrid will begin after a good night's sleep: I'll be starting early, finishing very late, and, this being the perfect pedestrian city, spending most of the day on foot.

### Breakfast

The only place for breakfast is the Ritz. It'll be just warm enough by nine to sit out in the garden terrace, by the fountain, summoning my energies with a powerful Cafe con leche, whilst waiters attend to my every need. If I were lucky enough to have a room upstairs, a perfect day might simply involve going back to bed. If I was staying across the road at the Palace, I'd probably do likewise.

### Morning

There's no escaping the art. With one of the richest collections in Europe, spread principally amongst the 'big three' museums, it's hard to know where to start. The secret is to plump for one, and leave the rest for another visit. I would go for the Reina Sofia, never passing up the chance for another look at Picasso's Guernica. On this vast monotone canvas lies the entire tragedy, horror and despair of the Spanish Civil War. Almost more shocking are the surrounding horrific, preparative drawings. After Dali, Miro, and three more floors of Spanish Modern art, it's probably time to get some fresh air. Just across the Calle Atocha lie the serene Botanical Gardens. Wandering past the simple sprinkling fountains and discarded rakes, I'll head for the vegetable patches, so fecund that signs have been erected warning local opportunists that under no circumstances may the produce be eaten. Which reminds me, it must be time for.....

## Lunch

Over the road on Calle Alcala is the Circulo de Bellas Artes, the Fine Arts museum. Despite impressive temporary exhibitions, I'm appalled to say that I only ever come for the bar. With high ceiling frescoes, that reclining marble nude, Grecian pillars, indulgent chandeliers, whispering conversation, and acres of breathing space, this is Madrid's most ethereal gallery bar, pure escapism. What's more, it does a very slightly sophisticated, and extremely delicious, three course Menu del Dia.

## Afternoon

Presuming I'm following the Madrileno timetable, it must be about three o'clock, which gives me over an hour to spare. Luckily I'm five minutes from the sprawling Retiro park, a good place to rest up under a tree and watch everyone heading back to work after lunch. Then, sometime towards five, I'll catch a cab across town to the Paseo del Pintor Rosales, where the Teleferico begins. This is Madrid's most random attraction, a rustic, ski-style bubble car that whisks you out over the city, past high apartment block windows, across the river and six lanes of traffic, into the Casa del Campo park. There's nothing more exciting at the other end than acres of empty park land and one invaluable commodity, the essence of perfection in the city of Madrid, silence.

Whether walking back to the city or risking the Teleferico again, I'll aim for Cafe de Oriente, on Plaza de Oriente, for a drink on the quiet terrace, looking across the square towards the Grand Palace. When the sun finally starts to sink, there's a great view next to the Palace entrance, out across the city's green outskirts, where the sun eventually sets. We must bid it fondly farewell, before things really get going.

Evening

In true Ritzy, perfect-day style, I'm meeting friends for supper at the Royal Opera House restaurant on Calle Felipe V (Tel: 91 516 0670). This is one of the most extravagant dining experiences in Madrid. Entered via a series of opulent, tapestry-draped halls, past life-size portraits of the king and queen, one is greeted by a small army of white-gloved personnel, before being fed beneath a star-encrusted ceiling. The food is rich, Spanish (the baby broad bean 'revuelto' and the local sirloin are favourites), and far from ridiculously expensive. Well fed, it's time to head for the bars up the road in La Latina. Cava Baja is a good street to start on, sipping Rioja at a couple of wine bars before climbing up to the top-floor roof-terrace at El Viajero, on Plaza de la Cebada, for great views across the old town's rooftops.

## THE END

No matter what time it is, a perfect night out in Madrid must end with 'chocolate con churros' at the legendary 'Chocolateria San Gines' on Plaza San Gines, followed, finally, by a last look at the Plaza Mayor. By now it's practically empty, serene, your own private Plaza, a perfect place for a moment's rest on the weary walk home.

BENJAMIN CURTIS, (EDITOR) escaped London for a month in 1998, wound up in Madrid, and has remained ever since. Originally a photographer, he took up writing in Spain, and is now so enamoured with the Spanish that he rarely travels, or writes about, anywhere else.

MAUREEN BARRY has contributed regular travel, food and wine features to BA Highlife magazine for twelve years, as well as contributing to other titles in the Premier group, national magazines and newspapers. She is a partner in an Internet Information company and writes regularly for the web. She holds a BA degree in Russian and French from London University and has one published novel, 'Brilliant'.

DAVID CLEMENT-DAVIES is a travel writer and novelist. He has written freelance pieces for most UK national broadsheets, contributes regularly to magazines and co-wrote 'The Insight Guide to Florence'. His first novel, 'Fire Bringer', was published by Macmillan Childrens Books. His stories have been translated into German, Italian and Japanese and have been published in Australia, Canada and America.

JAMES HENDERSON has contributed to the Travel Pages of the Financial Times and other broadsheets for the past ten years, and is author of The Cadogan Guide to the Caribbean, now in its fifth edition.

MARK HUDSON's first book, 'Our Grandmothers' Drums', won the Thomas Cook Award and the Somerset Maugham Award. His second, 'Coming Back Brockens', won the NCR Award for the best non-fiction book of 1995. A novel, 'The Music in my Head', was published to critical acclaim in 1998. He writes on travel for the Daily Telegraph, the Mail on Sunday and the Sunday Times.

JIM KEEBLE writes regularly for the travel pages of the UK's Daily and Sunday Telegraph, the Times and Sunday Times and the Evening Standard. His first book, 'Independence Day - Travels around America With a Broken Heart' was published by Abacus. He writes about anywhere that offers strange stories and frothy cocktails.

PHILIP MARSDEN's books include 'The Crossing Place; A Journey among the Armenians' (winner of the Somerset Maugham Award),

'The Bronski House' and 'The Spirit-Wrestlers and Other Survivors of the Russian Century' (winner of the Thomas Cook / Daily Telegraph Travel Book Award). He is a Fellow of the Royal Society of Literature and his work has been translated into nine languages.

KAMIN MOHAMMADI is an editor and writer based in London, where she settled many years ago after escaping a revolution. She has written guidebooks for Cadogan Guides and is a regular writer and reviewer for Geographical magazine and WEXAS Traveller as well as Condé Nast titles. She currently edits a stable of glossy magazines for Condé Nast. Her areas of expertise include Spain, Portugal, Iceland and Iran.

MELISSA ROSSI - aka "the gypsy with a laptop" - is a contributing editor for National Geographic Traveler and has been published in American magazines from Newsweek to Esquire. She has written several books, including a biography of Mrs Cobain, 'Courtney Love: Queen of Noise' (1996). She is currently in the Netherlands working on "The Armchair Diplomat" - a guide for the internationally illiterate and geographically challenged.

ANTHONY SATTIN is a writer, critic and broadcaster. He is the author of several books including a novel 'Shooting the Breeze', and the highly acclaimed 'The Pharaoh's Shadow', the subject of a Radio 4 documentary. He has written for television, radio and for numerous publications in the UK and abroad and is a regular contributor to the Sunday Times books and travel pages.

CHRISTOPHER SOMERVILLE is one of the UK's most respected freelance travel writers. His 'Walk of the Month' feature has been running in the Daily Telegraph for ten years, and his travel pieces appear regularly in Britain's top-quality newspapers - the Daily and Sunday Telegraph, the Times and the Sunday Times. Christopher has written around 20 books - some accounts of his travels, several walking guides, and guidebooks to the UK, Ireland and Crete. Broadcasting activity includes researching, writing and presenting his own long-running 'Somerville's Walks' series on TV, and a varied experience of radio which now includes presenting a monthly walk on BBC Radio 4's travel programme 'Excess Baggage'.

Jasper Winn is a writer, photographer, broadcaster and filmmaker with specialist interests in world music, horses, the peoples of remote regions, bizarre festivals, and anything off-beat. He writes regularly for The Evening Standard, CN Traveller, Geographical, The Times and The Independent on Sunday. He broadcasts for the BBC and RTE and has made and presented travel documentaries for C4. He is a frequent lecturer for the RSGS, The British Council and national travel shows.

Acknowledgements

*Riding in Spain* was first published in the Evening Standard; copyright Jim Keeble.
*Last Stronghold of the Moorish Kings* and *Galicia of the Celts* were first published in High Life Magazine; copyright Maureen Barry.
*A House in Spain* by Mark Hudson is published by kind permission of the Daily Telegraph.
*Walking in Andalusia* first published in the Daily Telegraph; copyright Philip Marsden.


Picture Credits. All images except p.104 © Benjamin Curtis
Page 17 Water Gardens in the Generalife, Alhambra Palace, Granada;
Page 18 La Concha Bay, San Sebastian;
Page 35 Gypsy Girls;
Page 36 Restaurant in the Plaza Mayor, Madrid;
Page 85 Santa Semana Procession, Seville;
Page; 86 Las Fallas, Valencia;
Page 103 Bolonia Beach, Costa de la Luz;
Page 104: Walking in the Pyrennees; © Walkabout Tours
Page 121 Picos de Europa, Asturias;
Page 122 Olive Groves, Andalusia;
Page 139 Wall Tiles, Alhambra Palace, Granada;
Page 140 Andrin Coast, Asturias;
Page 157 Village Church, Picos de Europa;
Page 158 Pilgrimage of La Virgin de la Cabeza, Andalusia;
Page 175 Cuenca Old Town, Castilla La Mancha;
Page 176 Altea Old Town, Costa Blanca;